TYRANNY AND RESISTANCE

TYRANNY AND RESISTANCE

THE MAGDEBURG CONFESSION
AND THE LUTHERAN TRADITION

DAVID M. WHITFORD

SAINT LOUIS

Copyright ©2001 David M. Whitford
Published by Concordia Publishing House
3558 S. Jefferson Avenue, Saint Louis, MO 63118-3968
Manufactured in the United States of America

Library of Congress Cataloging-in-Publication Data

Whitford, David M. (David Mark)
    Tyranny and resistance : the Magdeburg Confession and the Lutheran
tradition / David M. Whitford.
       p. cm.
    Includes bibliographical references and index.
    ISBN 0-570-01643-6
    1. Magdeburg Confession. 2. Government, Resistance to—Religious
aspects—Lutheran Church—History of doctrines—16th century. 3.
Government, Resistance to—Germany—History—16th century. 4. Lutheran
Church—Doctrines—History—16th century.   I. Title.
    BR355.M27 W48 2001
    261.7'092—dc21

                        2001002680

1   2   3   4   5   6   7   8   9   10   10   09   08   07   06   05   04   03   02   01

To Laurel and Abigail

CONTENTS

FOREWORD

David Whitford's study addresses the perennial cliché that Martin Luther was a "toady of the princes" whose theological ethics set in motion a German-specific pathos of obedience that inevitably led to Christian passivity before National Socialism. Such nonsense has had an incredibly long shelf life, stretching from Thomas Müntzer's shrill rhetoric and the failed apocalyptic convictions of the Peasants' War through Ernst Troeltsch's arguments that Luther split public and personal morality, thus disposing Lutheranism toward political absolutism. Within academe, Troeltsch's position has been perpetuated from Reinhold Niebuhr through Max Stackhouse. These charges have been popularized—in the worst sense of the term—by William Shirer's nearly omnipresent *The Rise and Fall of the Third Reich* and the recent "biography" of Luther by Richard Marius, *Martin Luther: The Christian between God and Death*.

Whitford debunks this received tradition that pictures Luther as the poster child for quietism at best and fascism at worst. He does so by solid historical-theological analysis of the pertinent Luther writings and an extended discussion of their influence on the seminal expression of theologically grounded resistance to authority—*The Magdeburg Confession* of 1550. This *Confession* by the Lutherans of Magdeburg, taken up by their followers who struggled to defend the freedom of the church against early German absolutism, was a significant influence on the subsequent theological-political resistance movements among Calvinists.

Whitford convincingly demonstrates both theologically and historically the direct connection between Luther's theology and *The Magdeburg Confession*. Both elements—the theological and the historical—of Whitford's argumentation are crucial. He recognizes that to focus only on Luther's Law-Gospel dialectic and the "two kingdoms" doctrine leaves the discussion on the level of abstraction, whereas to focus only on the historical development of political resistance fails to recognize the crucial significance of theology for politics. Whitford's recognition of the intimate relationship of theory and praxis is a salutary reminder of the importance of both to the contemporary life of the church. Without solid theological foundation and direction, the church will tend to take on the mores of its historical-social context; without a confession of faith, the church will have little to say in a time of crisis. On the other hand, without the Gospel-provided courage "to sin boldly," the message will remain under a bushel. It was, therefore, no accident that, when faced by National Socialism, church leaders of resistance turned to their 16th-century roots in the Reformation and *The Magdeburg Confession*. The outstanding example of this awareness of the tradition was Hans Christoph von Hase, whose retrieval of "in casu confessionis" ("In the situation in which a confession is required or which causes scandal, nothing is an indifferent matter.") was so significant to his cousin and confidant, Dietrich Bonhoeffer. The scandal to the Confessing Church was, of course, the National Socialist co-option of the church with the attendant subversion of the Gospel and the persecution of Jews.

Whitford's study does not, of course, provide a road map for traversing current and future socio-political issues and crises, but it does remind us that Luther's dialectic of Law and Gospel, as well as the Confessions of the Reformation, provide an invaluable compass for the churches' navigation in troubled waters.

—Carter Lindberg
Boston University

PREFACE

We are like dwarfs standing on the shoulders of giants; thanks to them, we see farther than they. Busying ourselves with the treatises written by the ancients, we take their choice thoughts, buried by age and human neglect, and we raise them, as it were from death to renewed life.—Peter of Blois (d. 1212)

When I began the search for a diamond engagement ring, I had never heard of the four C's or why they mattered. I had an amount I could spend and thought that was all that mattered. My first salesman set me straight.

There are four C's to diamonds, and they make all the difference: cut, clarity, color, and carat. Although not a C, facets make a big difference as well: The more facets, the more light refraction and the prettier—and costlier—the ring. Turning the ring, looking at different facets, is what makes a diamond sparkle. Without facets, all you have is a rock.

In this regard, people are like diamonds. If you look at only one facet of a person's life, you miss the depth, the complexity, the sparkle. For too long, people have looked at Luther's thought on political involvement from only one angle: Luther has been accused of fostering a quietist response to the government that is politically conservative at best and reactionary at worst. In this book, I examine Luther from another angle.

Luther could and, in fact, did engender an ethic of political involvement. Describing this facet of Luther gives needed depth and color to a portrait that is often drawn in sharp lines of black and white.

To demonstrate that the portrait of Luther as a Quietist (i.e., one who believes that the government must always be obeyed, whether it is right or wrong) is reductionary at best, we must examine the relationship between Luther's understanding of "what makes a Christian" (his phrase) and his view of Christian political involvement. In Luther, there is a connection between Christian identity and community action. Although his discussion is often focused on particular political or social situations, his understanding of the Christian as a political actor is the underlying motif guiding his thought.

This conclusion requires us to examine the impact of Luther's theology of the cross on his understanding of the individual as a Christian and of that person's political involvement. Then, in reference to *The Magdeburg Confession*, we will highlight the striking degree to which the authors of that work echo and reflect Luther's central concerns and thought.

The Reformation era in Germany was a time of definition and description. Luther and his followers had to define themselves not only negatively (i.e., in opposition to Rome), but also positively (i.e., highlighting what they stood for). Luther and his followers also had to defend themselves and their positions. Were they heretics? Were they insane? Were they just troublemakers? This work of definition, description, and defense was a process.

Here we shall chart one aspect of the process of description and defense within Lutheran circles: the right to resist constituted authority by lesser magistrates. I do not argue that their defense of resistance theology was the only concern for the Lutheran reformers. No one would deny that social and political contexts affected both Luther and the Magdeburg pastors. However, in each case they wrote not as political or social commentators, they wrote as pastors. Thus the doctrines they espouse and the justifications given to support those doctrines are integral to a proper understanding of their thought and actions. The choice to focus on the intellectual and theological motifs is a conscious decision because doctrine mattered in their lives.

This is not to say that there weren't other motives that helped sway people toward Luther. However, even then doctrine was decisive. In most cases, there were easier and more prudent courses of action one could follow to assure one's goals.[1] Politically speaking, siding with Luther was never a sure bet. These facts focus our attention on the descriptions and definitions that Luther and the pastors of Magdeburg used to bolster their position that evangelical preaching must be defended and that resisting those who sought to suppress it was allowable (even honorable).

A NOTE ON SOURCES AND TRANSLATIONS

The basic source for this study is the primary political writings of Luther.[2] Thus, attention focuses on his "Letter to the Princes of Saxony concerning the Rebellious Spirit," the *Torgau Declaration*, many of the letters to individual noblemen, and such major tracts as *Temporal Authority* and *Dr. Martin Luther's Warning to His Dear German People*. I also consulted Luther's commentaries and sermons on significant scriptural texts that deal with political themes.

The political resistance of the city of Magdeburg in 1550 represents a continuation—a concrete application—of Luther's thought. To advance this hypothesis, I shall undertake a complete and systematic exegesis of the Magdeburg *Bekenntnis*. To date neither a critical edition nor the original texts of the Magdeburg *Bekenntnis* exist. The earliest extant German edition is contained in a collection of writings associated with the German Wars of Charles V, published in 1615. The Latin text, *Si, Confessio et Apologia Pastorum et reliquorum Ministrorum Ecclesiæ*, is published in *Bibliographie Reconditae* (Amsterdam: P. Schippers, 1966), no. 370. No critical or authoritative English translations of the work have been published. I have made use of Dr. A. M. Stewart's unpublished translation, but I have felt free to edit it to reflect the original more accurately. The German edition of the text is 129 pages. For purposes of readability and style, the spelling and punctuation of early modern texts (e.g., *Bekenntnis* instead of *Bekentnis*) has been modernized, except when quoting directly from the original. Whenever practical, I have used Scripture quotations from the New Revised Standard Version (NRSV).

ACKNOWLEDGMENTS

Finally, the companions along the way make the road to any significant achievement easier. There are so many who have made this journey worth the trip. Dr. Carter Lindberg taught me not only about scholarship, but also about life and hope. When I began course work at Boston University, I did not intend to write on Luther. I am a United Methodist preacher's kid who went to Presbyterian Seminary, so maybe Wesley or even Calvin. But Luther?

Carter's appreciation for Luther is infectious, though, and after one course on Luther with him, I was hooked. I thank Carter for teaching me how to read Luther with an appreciative, yet critical, eye. Professors David Hempton, Barbara Diefendorf, and John Clayton helped me to tighten the arguments in this work through their questions and critiques. I thank them for an informative and not too horrific defense.

To Kenneth Wagener and the people at Concordia Publishing House I owe a great debt of gratitude. Ken's enthusiasm for this work, his patience in guiding it through the maze that is modern publishing, and his forbearance of my many phone calls and e-mails is greatly appreciated. I would also like to thank Dr. Douglas Johnson, chairperson of the Religion and Philosophy Department at Claflin, for making my transition from parish life to academic life a joy. Finally, I owe a debt of thanks to Dr. Vermelle

Johnson (vice president of Academic Affairs) and Dr. Henry Tisdale (president of Claflin) for giving me the opportunity to be a part of the Claflin family. I have been graciously welcomed and constantly encouraged.

I am grateful to Professor Alasdair Stewart for his permission to use and edit as I saw fit his translation of *The Magdeburg Confession*. Alasdair has proven to be a faithful friend and a friendly critic. The University of South Carolina Thomas Cooper Library's John Osman Collection of Braun and Hogenberg City Views has graciously allowed me to use their copy of the *City of Magdeburg*. The portrait of Martin Luther is from the Richard Kessler Reformation Collection at Emory University's Pitt Theological Library. I appreciate their permission to include it and the work that they do on behalf of Reformation studies. The rest of the images are from Max Geisberg's *German Single Leaf Woodcuts: 1500–1550* and appear courtesy of Hacker Art Books, Inc., New York.

My parents (Rev. Dr. Charles and Ann Whitford) provided me with an environment in which to grow that nurtured the heart and the mind. In my home growing up there were three larger-than-life figures who animated my father's stories of ethics, discipleship, and responsibility (while this may seem like strange dinner table topics to some, I think most preacher's kids will understand). They were: Martin Luther King Jr., Robert F. Kennedy, and, most important, Dietrich Bonhoeffer.

I was raised on the stories of the American civil rights movement, on the stories of the fight for justice, and on the admirable story of Bonhoeffer's commitment to Christ and his heroic opposition to Hitler. I owe much of my enthusiasm for theology and politics to my parents. To my mind, there is no one more interesting in both aspects than Luther. More directly, my father read every page of this work more than once. I am thankful for his encouragement and his support. He is, in part, responsible for making this work more readable; all errors remain mine.

But most important are Laurel and Abigail. Without the two of them, I could not do what I do. Laurel constantly encourages me in all that I do. I thank God each and every day for the gift of her love and her patience with me as I finished this work. Abigail fills my life with wonder and awe. She reminds me that life is a gift to be treasured. She also reminds me that playing outside is sometimes the most important thing to do in the world. Most fittingly, then, this book is dedicated to them.

—David Whitford
Orangeburg, South Carolina
Lent 2000

1

CHRISTIAN IDENTITY AND POLITICAL IDENTITY

In short, I will preach it, teach it, write it, but I will constrain no man by force, for faith must come freely without compulsion. Take myself for an example. I opposed indulgences and all the papists, but never by force. I simply taught, preached, and wrote God's Word; otherwise I did nothing. And while I slept, or drank Wittenberg beer with my friends Philip and Amsdorf, the Word so weakened the papacy that no prince or emperor ever inflicted such losses upon it. I did nothing; *the Word did everything.*—Martin Luther, *First Invocavit Sermon* (9 March 1522) (*emphasis added*)

PERSONAL IDENTITY IN RELATION TO WORLD-BUILDING

Most families have stories that they tell to their newest members to teach them what it means to be part of the family. The shared stories weave the tapestries of life together; children or new friends are "storied" into families. In his magisterial volume on the Reformation, Carter Lindberg intimately ties memory to personal identity and history to communal identity.[1]

A central tenet of this book is that our sense of self influences how we live in the community. The stories that we have been taught and the lessons that we have learned affect our sense of self and influence how we act in the public square. Even more, religion constructs or shapes large portions of our experience. In much the same way that language shapes our experience of reality, religion, too, shapes our experience of what is real.

Emile Durkheim (1858–1917) was one of the first to combine the study of religion and sociology. Durkheim noted that religion is "eminently social." Beyond the intuitively obvious—that religion has a social or communal aspect—Durkheim meant that religion helps to create and give cohesion to the social world.[2] Religious beliefs are the creations of the "collective effervescence" (or collective thought). Religion becomes ritualized around a totem as part of the separation of reality into two arenas: the sacred and the profane. These totems become manifestations of the collective's sacred. They become rallying signs. Religion, thus, attaches us to our community. It is what binds the community together.

Building on the work of Durkheim and others, Peter Berger, in his book *The Sacred Canopy*, makes the most direct connection between religion and world-building. We are born, Berger argues, unfinished.[3] To survive we must create social structures, we must create a world to live in. Religion plays a significant role in this process of world-building. It anchors that world. He writes:

> It can thus be said that religion has played a strategic part in the human enterprise of world-building. Religion implies the farthest reach of man's self-externalization, of his infusion of reality with his own meanings.[4]

The import of this theory of world-building is significant. This is especially true of the early Modern Era, during which religious conviction shaped large portions of people's entire lives.

Luther's theories on Christian identity and political discourse are studied not only to learn about the underlying structure of his theology in general, his theological presuppositions are studied, and should be studied, to ascertain how his theology supports or helps to create a particular worldview. In other words, how does Luther's specific understanding of Christian anthropology affect how a Christian ought to act in the public square? How does his understanding of Christian world-building differ from other answers to similar questions?

CHRISTIAN IDENTITY IN LUTHER

THE SEARCH FOR A GRACIOUS GOD

First and foremost, Martin Luther was a pastor. His need to proclaim the Word of God always affected his theological formulations and led him to address the social, political, and cultural context of his hearers.

An overarching crisis of meaning or value marked the late medieval period. By the middle of the 14th century, the bubonic plague had reached its height, leaving large areas desolate. Famine nearly always follows both wars and plagues, and this era was no exception. Urbanization and social dislocation only added more misery to the mix. One's physical existence was a torment day to day. But above the heads of the people hung a more terrible torment—eternal damnation.

The issue for Luther, then, was one of salvation. In many ways, Luther reflected the angst of his age. Sitting on the cusp of modernity, yet still closely tied to the medieval world, Luther's search for a gracious God was affected not only by the crises of the time, but also by the theological milieu in which he was raised and educated.[5]

After primary education in Magdeburg and Eisenach, Luther entered the University of Erfurt in 1501. Between 1501 and 1505, Luther studied the basic course for the master of arts degree that included grammar, logic, rhetoric, and metaphysics. The principal role that William of Ockham's theology and metaphysics held in Erfurt's curriculum was significant for Luther's theological development. Ockham challenged many of the theological assumptions developed during the preceding centuries.

Until the acid of anxiety and crisis ate away the foundations, the Christian world rested securely on the Being of God as expounded by Thomas Aquinas (d. 1274). Thomas reflected both the maturity and pinnacle of scholasticism, which represented a way of thinking rather than a particular theory. Thomistic scholasticism was ordered, rational, and synthetic. The way Thomas beautifully synthesized the witness of Scripture, the tradition of the church, and the philosophy of Aristotle in syllogisms is an example of the embodiment of scholasticism in Thomas.

Grounding all of life in the mind of God, Thomas placed the world in an understandable and reassuring context. In the hierarchy of Being that establishes justice, the church was understood as the connection between the secular and divine. However, as the crises of the late Middle Ages increased, this reassurance began to erode.

Recognizing the shortcomings of Thomas's system, William of Ockham cut away most of the ontological grounding of existence. In its place, Ockham posited revelation and covenant. The world does not need to be grounded in some artificial, unknowable ladder of Being. Instead, one must rely on God's faithfulness. We are contingent upon God alone.

Without the assurance of God's covenant of grace, this contingency would be terrible and unbearable. In terms of God's absolute power (*potentia absoluta*), God can do anything. He can make a lie the truth; he can make adultery a virtue and monogamy a vice. The only limit to this power is consistency—God cannot contradict his own essence. To live in a world ordered by whim would be terrible; one would never know if one was acting justly or unjustly. However, God has decided on a particular way of acting (*potentia ordinata*). God has covenanted with creation and committed himself to a particular way of acting.

While rejecting some of Thomas, Ockham did not reject the entire scholastic project. He, too, synthesized and depended heavily on Aristotle. This dependence becomes significant in the covenantal piety of justification. The fundamental question of justification is where does one find fellowship with God, i.e., how does one know one is accepted by God? The logic of Aristotle taught Thomas and Ockham that "like is known by like." Thus, union or fellowship with God must take place on God's level. How can persons attain this ascent to God? Practice.

All people are born, it was argued, with potential. Although all creation suffers under the condemnation of the fall of Adam and Eve, there remains a divine spark of potentiality, a *syntersis*. This potential must be actualized; it must be habituated. Habituation is important for both Thomas and Ockham; however, Ockham slightly modified Thomas, and that modification had important implications in Luther's search for a gracious God.

From Thomas's perspective, the divine spark is infused with God's grace, giving one the power to be contrite (*contritio*) and cooperate with God. This cooperation with God's grace merits God's reward (*meritum de condign*). However, Ockham asked an important question: If the process begins with God's infusion of grace, can it truly merit anything? His answer was a resounding no! Therefore, you should do the best *you* can. Doing your best, minimal as it is, will merit (*meritum de congruo*) an infusion of grace: *facienti quod in se est Deus non denegat gratiam* (God will not deny his grace to anyone who does what lies within him). Doing one's best meant rejecting evil and doing good.

Despite being plagued by temptations or deep-seated angst (*Anfechtungen*),[6] Luther threw himself into the work of doing good and rejecting evil. On July 17, 1505, Luther joined the Augustinian monastery of Erfurt.[7] The rigors of monastic life, he believed, would assuage his anxiety. The hardships would cleanse him from evil, and the regimen would open him up to doing good works.[8]

Yet the rigors proved empty and the regimen fruitless. Luther remained as convinced as ever that he was a miserable worm. No matter what his confessor and advisor, Johann von Staupitz, advised, nothing seemed to work. Luther was left unconvinced. Each avenue of hope only provided another road to despair. Confession would sooth the soul with the hope of absolution, but not for Luther. He was obsessed with whether he had met the necessary threshold of contrition. Yes, he was contrite, but was he contrite enough? Concerning this period in his life, Luther later wrote:

> When I was a monk, I made great effort to live according to the requirements of the monastic rule. I made a practice of confessing and reciting all my sins, but always with prior contrition; I went to confession frequently, and I performed the assigned penances faithfully. Nevertheless, my conscience could never achieve certainty but was always in doubt and said: "You could have done this correctly. You were not contrite enough. You omitted this in your confession."[9]

Nothing seemed to work—not the sacraments, not the saints, not the mystics. Assurance eluded Luther. Hope was nowhere to be found. Out of frustration one day, Staupitz told Luther, "Look here, if you expect Christ to forgive you, come in with something to forgive—parricide, blasphemy, adultery—instead of all these peccadilloes."[10]

Staupitz pointed Luther to Christ. He told the young man to study the wounds of Christ, and in those wounds he might finally find his hope. Although any breakthrough still lay in the distant future, Staupitz had planted a seed that would eventually bear fruit in Luther's life and theology. Luther, himself, appreciated Staupitz's contribution:

> If I didn't praise Staupitz, I should be a damnable, ungrateful, papistical ass . . . for he bore me in Christ. If Staupitz had not helped me out, I should have been swallowed up and left in hell.[11]

Although the seed had been planted, the road remained dim, foreboding, and long.

The road took Luther to Wittenberg, first as a student and then (after a brief trip to Rome) as a professor of theology. In 1513, he began his first lectures in what would become his life's central academic work—the Old Testament. From 1513 to 1515, Luther lectured on the Psalms. It is in these lectures that we see the first fruits of the new spirit planted by Staupitz some eight to 10 years earlier. These lectures start Luther on the long road to "Damascus."[12]

Luther's choice of the Psalms is significant because in his day it was common to consider the Psalms as the poetic words of Christ. For Luther, Christ was the hermeneutical key that unlocked the meaning of the

Psalter. As early as the preface to his lectures, Luther states that the Psalms are a "foreword of Jesus Christ."[13]

If Christ did indeed speak through the Psalms, then in the development of what would become Luther's theology of the cross, Psalm 22 plays a pivotal and important role. Psalm 22 is a hymn of lament and anguish. In the Gospels of Mark and Matthew,[14] Christ's last words from the cross quote its first line: "My God, my God, why have you forsaken me?"[15] The import of this was critical for Luther. Christ himself cried out from the cross words of abandonment and angst. Christ himself suffered *Anfechtungen!* The question that then confronted Luther, and continues to confront Christians today, is how could this be? How could the Son of God suffer alienation? How could the perfect and sinless Christ be abandoned? The answer is found in the atonement.

Luther modifies slightly yet profoundly Thomas Aquinas's reinterpretation of Anselm's satisfaction theory of the atonement.[16] In Anselm, sin is either punished or satisfaction is made. Aquinas combines the ancient ransom theory with Anselm's and holds that satisfaction for sin is made in the punishment of Christ—thus the penal substitutionary theory. Luther, like nearly all theologians after Thomas, accepted this combination. However, in Thomas, Christ remains an innocent man.[17] Luther modified this theory, noting that Christ, as humanity's substitute, died on the cross a sinner.[18]

For years, Luther was haunted by an image of Christ sitting on a rainbow, judging creation with his "terrible swift sword." Here in the lectures on the Psalms, a new picture comes into focus. As Bainton notes:

> Where, then, is the judge, sitting on the rainbow and condemning sinners? He is still the judge. He must judge, as truth judges error and light darkness; but in judging he suffers with those whom he must condemn and feels with them subject to condemnation. The judge upon the rainbow has become the derelict upon the cross.[19]

The focus on Christ's dereliction on the cross marks the beginning of Luther's emerging theology of the cross. Luther looked at other major themes in the Psalms throughout his lectures; however, the emphasis remained on salvation and damnation. Here at last, it seems, Luther's search for a gracious God begins to bear fruit. Christ is no longer wielding the sword of terror; instead, he is the suffering servant.

Yet the question of the appropriation of this graciousness to the sinner continued to plague Luther. God may indeed be gracious, but how do I, as a sinner, know God's grace is applicable to me? Luther would finally find the answer to that question in the next two series of lectures he gave in

Wittenberg. From 1515 to 1517, he focused on Paul, and it was in Paul that Luther would discover the *sine qua non* of his life and his life's work: *sola gratia*—we are justified by grace through faith alone.

Cover of pamphlet published in Magdeburg in 1549, which calls Luther the "Third Elijah." *Translation:* "Lo, I will send you the prophet Elijah before the great and terrible day of the Lord" (Malachi 4:5). Christ spoke concerning the last days in Matthew 24 that the "good news of the kingdom will be proclaimed throughout the world, as a testimony to the nations; and then the end come." Therefore, it is easy to understand that because the preaching of the Gospel of the Lord Jesus Christ has been renewed and has been spread throughout the whole world by the Third Elijah that Judgment Day is not far off.

THEOLOGIA CRUCIS AND JUSTIFICATION BY FAITH

Man between God and the Devil

While Luther's *theologia crucis* certainly developed during these formative years, we must not underestimate the drama and importance of Luther's "tower" experience. Similar to the experience of the thunderstorm, the tower was a confirming and energizing moment in the life of Luther. In the tower, Luther discovered the righteousness of God, a gift, in Luther's words, of the Holy Spirit.[20]

The tower discovery overturned much of what Luther had been taught. His experience undermined much of the theology and piety of the late medieval period. It obliterated a theology of glory and began the dramatic move to a theology of the cross. Heiko Oberman rightly notes the drama of the moment:

> Must the trail of the Reformation be followed this far? There is a dignified way out: by cloaca Luther did not mean the toilet, but the study up in the tower above it. That, however, would be to miss the point of Luther's provocative statement. The cloaca is not just a privy, it is the most degrading place for man and the devil's favorite habitat. Medieval monks already knew this, but the Reformer knows even more now: it is right here that we have Christ, the mighty helper on our side. No spot is unholy for the Holy Ghost; this is the very place to express contempt for the adversary through trust in Christ crucified.[21]

The cloaca is a vivid representation of the revolution of the theology of the cross. God will not be placed in a box by mortal human beings. God is often revealed in the places one least expects to find him.

What was the revelation Luther discovered? In his "autobiography" written in 1545 (as the preface to his collected works in Latin), Luther writes:

> At last, by the mercy of God, meditating day and night, I gave heed to the context of the words, namely, "In it the righteousness of God is revealed, as it is written, 'He who through faith is righteous shall live.' " *There I began to understand that the righteousness of God is that by which the righteous lives by a gift of God, namely by faith.* And this is the meaning: the righteousness of God is revealed by the Gospel, namely, the passive righteousness with which merciful God justifies us by faith, as it is written, "He who through faith is righteous shall live." Here I felt that I was altogether born again and had entered paradise itself through open gates. There a totally other face of the scripture

showed itself to me. Thereupon I ran through the Scriptures from memory. I also found in other terms an analogy as, the work of God, that is, *what God does in us*, with which he makes us strong, the wisdom of God, with which he makes us wise, the strength of God, the salvation of God, the glory of God.[22]

Luther had not yet completely discovered "justification by faith alone," but he had unearthed it from its tomb of false assurances and vacuous indulgences. Philip Watson likens its significance to Copernicus's revolution. As much as Copernicus challenged contemporary thought regarding a geocentric world,[23] Martin Luther challenged the prevalent anthropocentric soteriology.[24] Instead of storehouses of merit, indulgences, habituation, and "doing what is within one," God accepts the sinner despite the sin. Acceptance is based on who one is in Christ rather than what one does. Justification is bestowed rather than achieved. Justification is not based on human righteousness, but on God's righteousness—revealed and confirmed in Christ.

In St. Paul, Luther finally found a word of hope and assurance; he discovered the graciousness of God. The discovery of God's graciousness *pro me* (for me) revolutionized all aspects of Luther's life and thought. From now on, Luther's response to the trials of his life and the crises of the late medieval period was to be certain of God but never to be dependent on human society. A tautology of Luther's theology becomes: One must always "let God be God." This frees human beings to be human. We do not have to achieve salvation; rather, it is a gift to be received. Thus, salvation is the presupposition of the life of the Christian and not its goal. This belief engendered Luther's rejection of indulgences and his movement to a *theologia crucis*.[25]

For Luther, the *theologia crucis* meant a judgment against all preconceived notions of God. It meant that theology was *fides quaerens intellectum* and never the reverse.[26] This conclusion led Luther to reject Aristotle as theological prolegomena because it is never possible to begin with human wisdom and arrive at God.[27] The only way to God is in God's own self-revelation. That step led Luther to become a theologian of the Word of God.

Verbum Domini Manet in Æternum[28]

Luther's theology of the Word can be summed up in the short phrase, "Scripture holds Christ like a cradle." In his "Preface to the Old Testament," Luther states that in Scripture

you will find the swaddling cloths and the manger in which Christ lies, and to which the angel points the shepherds. Simple and lowly are these swaddling cloths, but dear is the treasure, Christ, who lies in them.[29]

Luther's hermeneutic of the Word is a hermeneutic of Christ-centeredness. Because Luther is primarily concerned with proclaiming the testament of God's graciousness, he most clearly sets forth as the center of Scripture those texts that announce God's redemption of humanity.

This incarnational framework also undergirds Luther's understanding of preaching. Christ is the incarnate Word, the incarnation of proclamation. For the salvation of humanity it is more important to proclaim the Word than simply to read the Word. This is the idea that lies behind the reformation dictum, *fides ex auditu* (faith comes through hearing). When reading, the reader can remain separate from the words being read; there is a distance. This is far less possible in proclamation. In conversation it is very difficult to remain distant; when someone is speaking to you, it is difficult to ignore him or her. While one may look away, it is harder to "hear away."

For Luther, a proper theology of proclamation was not possible without the *theologia crucis*. Luther's theology of the Word of God affects both his anthropology and his political theology because it is based not in speculation or philosophical principles, but in revelation. Unlike scholastics who saw continuity between revelation and perception, Luther notes that revelation must be indirect and concealed.

Because of humanity's fallen condition, one can neither understand the redemptive word nor see God face-to-face. Here Luther's exposition on thesis 20 of his "Heidelberg Disputation" is important. He alludes to Exodus 33, where Moses seeks to see the glory of the Lord but instead sees only the backside. No one can see God face-to-face and live, so God reveals himself on the backside, that is to say, where it seems he should not be. For Luther this meant the human nature of Christ, in his weakness, his suffering, and his foolishness.[30]

Thus revelation is seen in the suffering of Christ rather than in moral activity or political constructs. It is addressed to faith, "which alone recognizes it as a revelation *of God*."[31] This is, in brief, Luther's doctrine of the *Deus absconditus*. The revelation of redemption in Jesus Christ is both a hiddenness in revelation and a revelation in hiddenness.

Luther's concern was with subjective anthropocentric speculative theology that began with humanity as the *a priori*. In philosophy, moral law, or history, humanity was the starting point for thinking about God. Luther absolutely rejected this. Biblical and evangelical theology must operate from above to below, that is to say, from God's self-revelation to us, not from us to God. This, in other words, was Luther's complete rejection of a *theologia gloriae*.

Theologia Gloriae

As a preacher and pastor now convinced of God's graciousness and the need to preach that gracious gift in Christ, Luther confronted one of the first trials of his tower experience in the fall of 1517. Johann Tetzel of Leipzig, the most famous and most successful indulgence evangelist of the day, appeared near Wittenberg. Indulgences were a manifestation, Luther believed, of everything that was wrong with the church. They embodied the *theologia gloriae* and all human efforts to earn salvation.[32]

Indulgences began in much the same manner as did Luther's reformation. They were initiated as a pastoral care response to soothe the consciences of people uncertain of their salvation. Theologically, their justification rested in Anselmian atonement theory. Indulgences were meant to satisfy the rigors of penance. As a sinner, one must first be contrite in coming before God and his priest. Then the sinner must honestly confess the sin. These two acts remove the guilt or stain from the sinner's heart. But what about God's justice? In his righteousness, God has been offended by this sin; his righteousness demands satisfaction. It is penance that satisfies God's righteousness and commutes the penalty.

Why did Luther reject indulgences? Instead of fostering dependence on God, indulgences placed "salvation" in the hands of traveling salesmen who hawked forgiveness like snake oil. Luther rejected all types of theology that were based in models of covenant. Indulgences, in a real sense, promoted a *do ut des* (I give that you may give) approach to God's mercy.

Luther's tower experience, his break with the *via moderna*, and his repudiation of indulgences all pointed away from theologies of covenant. Convenant theologies, he recognized, attempt to put God in a box. They are rooted in "if then" language. If I do x, then you must do y.[33] Luther rejected this type of legalism. Second, the presence of "If I" in models of covenant places the onus of salvation on the subject, largely excluding God from the discussion.

The import of the tower experience was the discovery that God's righteousness is a gift received passively by humankind and that evangelical theology affirms God's testament in Christ. From the author of Hebrews,[34] Luther took an understanding of Jesus Christ as the last will and testament of God.[35] God has written humanity in the will as heirs of God and co-heirs with Christ. The import of testament, though, is that the testate must be dead for the will to be in effect. So if a person is in the will, she is included; but if she is not written in, no matter how much she strives, no matter what works of supererogation she does, she will not be included. It is, then, no coincidence that Luther wrote in the treatise *The Freedom of a Christian* that salvation is not the goal of life—that is, Christians are not trying to satisfy some "if then" statement. Rather, faith is the foundation of life—its presupposition.[36]

The rejection of covenant model theologies and the movement to testament is a fundamental aspect of Luther's *theologia crucis*. It is a repudiation of any type of *theologia gloriae* with a profound impact on Luther's anthropology of a Christian. First and foremost, Luther disavows "all efforts to ascend to God whether they be speculative, ethical, or experiential."[37] The Reformer makes a small but significant alteration of Augustinian anthropology. In that system, human beings are *partim bonum, partim malum* or *partim iustus, partim peccator* (partly good/just, partly bad/sinner). The *goal* of a Christian's life is to grow in righteousness. In other words, one must work to decrease the side of the equation that is bad and sinful. As one decreases the sin in oneself, the good and just aspect of one's being increases.

Luther's anthropology, however, is an outright rejection of this view of progress. Whether understood ethically, experientially, or mystically, progress is a work and thus must be rejected. Luther's alternative characterization of Christian anthropology was *simul iustus et peccator* (at once righteous and sinful.) He speaks of righteousness in two ways: *coram deo* (before God) and *coram hominibus* (before man). Instead of a development in righteousness based in the person, or an infusion of merit from the saints, a person is judged righteous before God because of the work of Christ. But absent the perspective of God and the righteousness of Christ—based on one's own merit—a Christian still looks like a sinner.[38]

Law and Gospel

One of the more complex aspects of Luther's theology of the cross is his distinction between the Law and the Gospel. In his book *Theology of the Reformers*, Timothy George noted three persistent characteristics in Luther's theology: It "was at once *biblical, existential,* and *dialectical.*"[39] Nowhere is that more true than in Luther's understanding of the Law and the Gospel.

Existentially, the distinction between Law and Gospel grew out of Luther's search for a gracious God and the need as pastor to share his rediscovery of God's grace with others who shared the same basic yearning: How do I know that I am loved and accepted by God? The proper distinction between Law and Gospel involves nothing less than justification.[40]

The Law and Gospel are a central dialectic in Luther's thought. This distinction does not mean that they are simply antithetical; the Law is not replaced or excluded by the Gospel. The Law is not synonymous with the Old Testament nor is the Gospel synonymous with the New Testament. They are dialectical and complementary. The Law and the Gospel must be understood without confusion or division. To set aside the Law would (as Anselm pointed out) jeopardize God's justice and righteousness; to set aside the Gospel jeopardizes God's grace and love. Viewed from God's perspective, both Law and Gospel serve his justice and are gifts of his grace and love—God gives them both to us for our salvation. Both are needed.

From the perspective of creation, though, Law is experienced as judgment and restriction. So how does the Law aid God's plan of salvation? Luther notes especially two proper uses of the Law: the natural/civil/or political use and the theological. The first use of the Law is an aid to creation because it limits human sin and avarice and promotes the common good. Therefore, it functions as part of God's plan for ordering creation.

The Law is part of God's plan to limit the chaos inflicted on creation by the devil. The devil and evil are limited by actual laws enforced by government[41] and by practical rules and regulations enforced and instantiated by parents, advisors, teachers, etc. The Law in its political sense is a good gift of God given to establish civil society. "Although the Law cannot make men good, so that they freely and willingly do all that it requires, it can control their behavior and prevent them from giving free rein to their contrary impulses."[42]

In its theological use, the Law reveals the utter uselessness and futility of salvation by works. If politically the Law is experienced as limit, here it is experienced as judgment. It condemns sin and kills the sinner so he or she may then come alive in Christ through the Gospel.[43] It is, therefore, a "helpmate" to the Gospel:

> Now, when sins are unrecognized, there is no room for a remedy and no hope of a cure; men will not submit to the touch of a healer when they imagine themselves well and in no need of a physician. Therefore, the Law is necessary to make sin known so that when its gravity and magnitude are recognized, man in his pride who imagines himself well may be humbled and may sigh and gasp for the grace that is offered in Christ.[44]

Understood properly, the Law is an *aid* to salvation. A real danger exists, however, when one misunderstands the proper use of the Law and confuses Law with Gospel.

When Law is confused with the Gospel and understood as a way of salvation, it becomes a tyrant and a terror. (Luther suffered under this misapprehension when he viewed God only as a terrible judge.) It is a tyrant because the demands of the Law are strict and the bar is held impossibly high. Constant vigilance is the only remedy, and such vigilance is unattainable.

Therefore, if the Law were once an "avenue" to salvation, sin has shut it off. We have been left to our own devices and have come up short. The Law becomes a terror because it cannot effect our salvation. Despair rules when the Law is confused with Gospel because there is no way to find a gracious God when the Law alone rules. Hope is found only in the Gospel of the crucified Christ. Gerhard Forde notes that whereas Law is spoken in imperative speech—"Thou shalt not murder"[45]—the Gospel comes to us in declarative statements: "There is therefore now no condemnation for those who are in Christ Jesus."[46]

> The difference between the old and the new, therefore, is a difference in *preaching*, a difference in how we speak to one another and on what authority we do so. . . . Those who do not understand this difference in speaking *do not understand the Gospel* . . .[47]

The Gospel, then, is the good news that God accepts a sinner as a forgiven saint, that sin has been washed away by the atoning sacrifice of Christ.

For the theologian and the preacher, this distinction between Law and Gospel is essential. When Law is confused with Gospel, it leads only to torture of the soul. When the Gospel is confused with the Law, this distorts a gift into a more severe requirement.[48]

For Luther, the Gospel becomes the foundation of one's new life in Christ. The distinction between Law and Gospel provides the shape and content of Luther's political theory: the doctrine of the two realms.

The Secular Realm and the Spiritual Realm

From the moment that Constantine converted to Christianity and conscripted his armies into the church to win a decisive battle, the church and the state have existed in an often unhealthy tension. Each tried to wield power and influence in the other's sphere. At Canosa in 1077, the emperor of the Holy Roman Empire was made to wait in the snow, pleading for absolution from Pope Gregory VII (Hildebrandt, d. 1085). In

1533, Henry VIII of England, by act of Parliament, pronounced himself "Supreme Head of the Church."

In *Divine and Human Authority in Reformation Thought*, Ralph Keen outlines three broad approaches within the Reformation to the relationship between the secular world and the spiritual: inclusively ecclesial, exclusively biblical, and inclusively biblical.[49] Hildebrandt at Canosa characterizes an *inclusively ecclesial* perspective: Authority for the governance of creation is founded by God in the church. God's authority flows to the church (and especially the pope); the church then yields some of that authority to the emperor. As far back as Pope Leo's bold move to crown Charlemagne emperor of the Romans (A.D. 800), Leo began the establishment of papal supremacy over secular authority.

The radical reformers developed an alternative approach. In the *exclusively biblical* model, the church must conform to the Gospel explicitly. No deviation is allowed. The relationship between the secular and spiritual is antagonistic. This antagonism seems to elicit two responses: withdrawal or usurpation. In many Anabaptist groups, the church withdrew from secular society and placed itself over and against the dominant culture. In some respects, this model is a resurrection and modification of the ecclesial model. The church must conform to the *whole* Bible, and the state must as well. Both Andreas Bodenstein von Karlstadt and Thomas Müntzer fall into this category. While Keen identifies biblicism as the fundamental source for this perspective, this perspective actually grows out of the group's understanding, based on the Bible, of Christian identity.

The third approach differs significantly from both the inclusively ecclesial and exclusively biblical models. Often labeled *magisterial*, the *inclusively biblical* approach is epitomized by Luther's doctrine of the two realms.[50] In Luther's thought, each realm is part of God's plan for ordering creation. The spiritual realm is eternal and everlasting; it is the realm of revelation and faith. Instantiated in the church, it exists to offer the grace of God to all through preaching the Word of God and celebrating the sacraments. It is, in a way, a foretaste of the heavenly banquet.

Two motifs run through Luther's thought about the spiritual realm: freedom and equality. Freedom enables one to act on the behalf of others. We are perfectly free from human obligations that we might serve others.[51] Revolutionary in this understanding is the revision of status. The spiritual realm is not governed hierarchically; in this realm, all Christians are equal. Luther writes:

> All Christians are truly of the spiritual estate, and there is no differ-
> ence among them except that of function. Paul says in 1 Corinthians
> 12.12–13 that we are all one body, with every member having his or
> her own function by which he or she serves the others. This is because
> we have one baptism, one Gospel, and one faith, and are all Christians
> just the same as each other; for baptism, Gospel, and faith alone make
> us spiritual and a Christian people . . . it follows from this argument
> that there is no true, basic difference between laymen and priests,
> princes and bishops, between religious and secular, except for the sake
> of office and work, but not for the sake of status.[52]

Since in Baptism there is no longer Jew nor Greek, slave nor free, in the
spiritual realm there are no distinctions of class or authority. As Jesus
explained to his disciples in Matthew 20, in the spiritual kingdom service
to others, not status, is definitive.

Like the Law to the Gospel, the secular realm is the spiritual realm's
dialectical partner; it is the realm of reason and unbelief. Both the secular
and spiritual exist for God's regulation of creation, but like Law and
Gospel, they play different roles. Whereas the spiritual realm is eternal
and proleptic, the secular is finite and fleeting.[53] Here the sword instead of
service is definitive.

Just as the Law serves God by enlightening persons to their sinful condition and thus prepares them for the proclamation of the Gospel, the secular realm limits the outbreak of sin and malfeasance and thus creates a cli-
mate where the Gospel can be preached. With this understanding, St. Paul
urged "that supplications, prayers, intercessions, and thanksgivings be
made for everyone, for kings and all who are in high positions, so that we
may lead a quiet and peaceable life in all godliness and dignity" (1 Tim
2:1–2). The secular realm orders the communal life—in the home, in the
city, and in the state. It ensures that the unjust will not run rampant over
the weak and downtrodden.[54]

Thus, Luther attempted to set a new course in the relationship
between the church and the state. He believed that God had constructed
government and other institutions among men and, consequently, complete obedience was due to God alone. With this shift in theology, Luther
reasoned that no one could claim complete and absolute authority but
God. Instead of one being the subject of the other, they each are to have
clearly defined roles and spheres of influence. The simple wisdom to the
doctrine of the two kingdoms is that "church leaders make poor kings, and
kings make poor bishops."[55] When one attempts to interfere in the realm

of the other, disaster is the usual outcome. Therefore, the two realms must remain distinct; to confuse them is comparable to the authorities of Leipzig passing laws for Wittenberg or vice versa.[56]

When secular authorities attempt to rule the realm of the sacred, the Gospel and salvation are put at risk. The rulers place themselves on the throne of God by deciding what is right and worthy of worship. They replace God's Word with human words and thereby drive "souls to eternal death."[57] To make matters worse, this kind of program is all in vain. Salvation and the things of God's kingdom are gifts to be freely received. They cannot be coerced or bought. The state may demand outward conformity, but it can never convert the will or the heart.

Luther's point, though seemingly obvious today, was nevertheless revolutionary for his time. God has given the secular prince the power of the sword for the maintenance of order and justice. That calling in itself is a high and worthy office. The magistrate—whether king, duke, burgher, or father—should devote himself to that calling and leave the proclamation of the Word and the disposition of souls to God and the church.

Likewise, the church ought to leave the maintenance of public order to the state and the confutation of heresy to the Word. Luther saw two fundamental dangers in attempts by the sacred realm to use the secular for its own ends. Either it makes the Gospel a new and more severe Law or it sentimentalizes the Law and thus weakens it. In the first instance, what ought to be "governed" by freedom is now ruled by force and coercion, corrupting the Gospel and destroying its message of grace. In the second case, the church, in seeking to supplant the state, underestimates the power of sin and malfeasance. The world is populated with sinners and the wicked. The just are a minority. In such a place, Luther notes, the Gospel will not be able to be preached because there will be no order or justice. The Reformer adds wryly, "Take heed and first fill the world with real Christians before you attempt to rule it in a Christian and evangelical manner."[58]

For Luther, the issue ultimately is one of trust. One must trust God and God's order of creation. The church has been given a special and unique role: the proclamation of the Gospel and the administration of the sacraments. It must trust God and the power of the Word. When the church trusts God and lives its life in the spiritual realm, it is free from alien responsibilities such as propping up governmental structures or endorsing certain societal mores. These political and cultural actions are not its responsibility; when the church embraces these actions, its message becomes confused.

The state, likewise, must recognize and use God's gift: the sword that maintains order. When it does, it is free to ensure justice and lawfulness, instead of hunting otherwise lawful heretics.

Each kingdom is entrusted with a special responsibility; while complementary, the two realms are nevertheless distinct. This distinction, Luther asserts frequently, must be maintained. A related question, however, is whether one can be a political agent and remain a Christian. Moreover, what options are open to the Christian when either the state or the church oversteps its bounds?

Conclusion

The Word of God, revealed in and through the Law, enlightens us to our true situation. We may believe that we have free will, that we lead good lives, and that we can achieve salvation on our own terms, but the Word shatters that illusion. Through the Law, we learn that we are helpless sinners bound to sin, death, and the devil.

Yet God does not leave us abandoned in this plight. Through the cross of Christ, the righteousness of God has been made available to all through faith. The issue for Luther, then, was justification. The crises of the time, combined with the theological heritage of late medieval Europe, led to Luther's own angst (or, as he described it, *Anfechtung*). This started him on his search for a gracious God. Luther's response to these crises was that Christians may be certain of God and his power to save, but they can never be secure in human society. This understanding led Luther to his rejection of indulgences and to his movement to a *theologia crucis*.

At stake in the *theologia crucis* is justification by grace through faith alone. Luther turned medieval theology and piety on its head by maintaining the view that one could be righteous *coram deo* yet appear unrighteous *coram hominibus*. This understanding is opposed to medieval pietistic theology (summarized in the slogan *facere quod in se est*), which held that righteousness *coram deo* is dependent on becoming like God, which outwardly reflects itself in a righteousness *coram hominibus*. For Luther, salvation is not "the process or goal of life, but rather its presupposition."[59]

Because salvation is the presupposition of the Christian life, the Christian possesses three types of freedom: from divine wrath, from the Law, and from human laws and traditions. The basic guide for right behavior is the law of love, i.e., the believer motivated by the indwelling Spirit of God. We act in love so as to benefit our neighbors. "In sum, everything not commanded by God is made a matter of freedom. Human laws may be observed or ignored freely so long as the love of neighbor is not violated."[60]

Given this freedom, the *theologia crucis* exerts a profound influence on Christian anthropology. First, security is found only in God and his revelation. Second, this revelation is veiled and, therefore, apprehended only by faith. Third, because of the hiddenness of revelation, one can appear to be unrighteous yet be righteous.

All these qualities have significant implications for political life and interaction. Because Luther believed security is found in God alone, political and social structures are only preliminary. They are not "ontological entities derived from the mind of God, but rather human structures to be worked out for the well-being of the neighbor."[61] While government exists to ensure justice and the freedom to preach the Gospel, it need not conform to the Gospel. In fact, Luther states that "it is not necessary for [the king] to be a Christian to rule."[62] This is the main implication of Luther's two kingdom's doctrine.

For Luther, history is veiled. *Deus absconditus* is a key interpretive principle in the Reformer's thought. Because God is revealed in hiddenness and hidden in revelation, it is not possible to use reason to state that God is "here" and not "there." It is difficult, if not impossible, for Christians to ordain political figures or events.[63]

Third, Luther clearly asserts that God is God. Human beings are frail, limited, and captured by sin. They cannot question the whirlwind or know the course of God's hand through history. Only God knows and directs the course of human events. To attempt to sit in that place usurps God's rightful place. We must let the Word do it all; anything else distrusts God and interferes in God's domain.

The folly of this attempt is demonstrated when double righteousness is added to the mix. The very authority (*Obrigkeit*) that seems so unjust and wicked from our perspective (*coram hominibus*) may, in fact, be an agent of God's judgment and wrath and, therefore, be righteous (*coram deo*).

Luther's position, of course, was not the only one in 16th-century Europe. Luther attempted to free both the church and state from undue influence by the other. Many contemporaries, however, disagreed with him on this point of engagement or cooperation between state and church. Almost immediately, Luther faced serious challenges to his views—first by Andreas Karlstadt, then by Thomas Müntzer.

2

THEORY BECOMES PRAXIS

THE PEASANTS' WAR AND THE AUGSBURG RECESS

If this plan or this undertaking is of human origin, it will fail; but if it is of God, you will not be able to overthrow them. (Acts 5:38–39)

As to the peasants and plebeians, they grouped themselves around the revolutionary party whose demands and doctrines found their boldest expression in Müntzer.—Frederick Engels, *The Peasant War in Germany*

SEMPER REFORMANDA

Philip Watson equated Luther's revolution to that of Copernicus because Copernicus, too, stood the known or understood world on its head. In another sense, however, Luther's reformation might more aptly be compared to Albert Einstein's revolution in quantum physics and theory.[1] In *Protestants: The Birth of a Revolution*, Steven Ozment expands on and demonstrates the numerous ways in which Luther's theories revolutionized medieval life: marriage, education, status and role of women and children, and many other arenas of human life.[2] One event within this political and social transformation was the German Peasants' War of 1525.

The Wittenberg revolution of 1517 and its energy affected all aspects of life: social structures, political allegiances and powers, economic systems, and ecclesiastical traditions. In 1521, Martin Luther was called to account for his theological "innovations" at the Diet of Worms. At Worms, as earlier at Heidelberg and Leipzig, Luther refused to recant his opinions unless he could be shown by Scripture or reason they were wrong.

On May 25, 1521, Emperor Charles V officially banned Luther, branding him an outlaw throughout the Holy Roman Empire. Overnight

Luther became a hunted man. The Saxon Elector Frederick the Wise diplomatically sought a solution to the Luther problem. While maintaining "viable deniability," Frederick had Luther "kidnapped" and secreted away to the Wartburg Castle.

Luther's isolation at the Wartburg assured his safety. It also, however, contributed to wild and intensifying rumors of his abduction and death. This created a leadership vacuum in Wittenberg. Andreas Karlstadt and the Zwickau prophets came to fill the void, precipitating the first real crisis of the Reformation.

Andreas Karlstadt was teaching in Wittenberg when Luther posted his Ninety-five Theses. A recognized Thomist scholar of his day, Karlstadt soon abandoned his Thomism and began to support and defend Luther. His new theological perspective differed from Luther's in one major sense: While Luther's theology is best defined as a theology of grace, Karlstadt's theology was a revised or updated perspective on the Law.[3] Luther's Christian anthropology is best defined by the phrase *simul iustus et peccator*; Karlstadt's anthropology is one of regeneration. For Karlstadt, the sinner through the power of God's grace is regenerated. Transformation from a life of sin to a life of holiness is integral to Karlstadt's understanding of Christian identity.

Luther's disagreement with Karlstadt had little to do with the types of reform or the speed of implementation of reforms. Luther found fault in *how* the reforms were implemented and why. Luther himself had argued for communion to the laity in both kinds, was indifferent about images, and had an openness to clerical marriage. Karlstadt's reforms were not the problem. His timing was poor, but even that was not the defining issue.

For Luther, all of these reforms were *opportunities* for the congregation, not *commands*. In contrast, Karlstadt's understanding of Christian identity led him to believe and teach that these reforms were mandatory rather than optional. Karlstadt believed they were part and parcel *of the Gospel*. For Karlstadt, because the church consists of the regenerate, it must conform to the Gospel as a new Law. Further, because he was convinced that his reforms were true to the Gospel, those who accepted his reforms were by definition the regenerate. The inverse also holds: Those who rejected the reforms were the reprobate. Such distinctions were impossible for Luther. The *theologia crucis* confounds all human attempts to put God into a box.

In many ways, this difference in theology defined the difference between Luther and Karlstadt in regard to the implementation of reform and foreshadows the more serious crisis of the Peasants' War. Luther's response to each crisis is essentially the same. Both Karlstadt and Müntzer attempt to implement church reform by force. For Luther this aborted the entire program. Force connotes coercion, and the Gospel is not about coercion, it is about grace.

Luther responded to the "Wittenberg Disturbances" with his famous *Invocavit Sermons.* The distinction that Luther made in his preaching and writing would play itself out throughout his life and his theology; it also continued to play a significant role in the theology of *The Magdeburg Confession.* The distinction Luther makes in the *Invocavit Sermons* is between the Law and the Gospel. When the Gospel (or church reforms) are transformed from gifts to requirements, the essence of the Gospel is sacrificed and abandoned. Regardless of how noble the reform, if it is forced on someone's conscience, it is not a reform at all, but a new law.

Karlstadt's actions in Wittenberg were raucous, iconoclastic, yet rather limited in scope and scale. He said the Mass in German, celebrated communion in both kinds, and encouraged clerical marriage. Far more threatening to the social fabric than Karlstadt's practices and with far more disastrous results was the "Revolution of the Common Man" (the Peasants' War) of 1525.[4]

Like those before them in Wittenberg, the peasants tapped into the tremendous energy unleashed by the Reformation. Undeniably, their perception of Luther's theology supported and, in their minds, justified their rebellion. Was their appropriation of Luther legitimate, however? Luther wrote vehemently against the revolt. The central distinction determining Luther's position on this political and social event was the theology of the cross and Christian identity.

THE PEASANTS' WAR AND THOMAS MÜNTZER

Although the Peasants' War had roots stretching back for decades, for all intents and purposes it "was primarily a phenomenon of about twenty-four weeks from late January to mid-July 1525."[5] The first period of the war was largely nonviolent. It reflected the dissatisfactions of peasants, of the emerging middle class in the towns, and of some disenfranchised nobles. This early phase—driven as it was by economic, political, and religious demands of the disenfranchised—had direct antecedents in the *Bundschuh* Revolt of 1493. According to Peter Blickle, many of the peasants' actions had more in common with a general strike than an outright rebellion.[6]

In the winter of 1525, the tide began to turn during the carnival season preceding Lent. Carnival events were—and are to this day—a mixture of popular piety, religious rite, and raucous celebration. The combination of the carnival atmosphere and the rising discontent among the peasants fed the rebellion.

The demands of the peasants were solidified in the *Twelve Articles* issued in late March or early April 1525.[7] The *Articles* were a response to critics who blamed the peasants for revolting and for abandoning the Gospel. The peasants asserted that both accusations were false. To the contrary, they claimed the Gospel as their own and sought to use the Bible as an arbiter of their grievances. In a veiled threat, they reminded the authorities that God heard the cries of the Israelites in Egypt and that God would hear their cries as well.

In using the Bible as standard and norm for the life of the community, the peasants hoped to connect their program with that of the Wittenberg reformation. Their *Articles* are full of marginal references to applicable Scripture proof texts. The *Articles* are actually 12 demands that point to the peasants' rebellion and war as an economic, political, and religious event. The line between religious demands and political or economic demands is blurred almost completely.

First, the peasants demanded the right to call their own pastors. Instead of having the pastor assigned by a bishop, the community ought to be able to call and release its pastor. The standard for any evaluation would be the pastor's adherence to the "pure and clear" Gospel. This demand in itself was revolutionary because it overthrew episcopal authority and centuries of tradition.

The second demand was just as explosive. It supported the Old Testament call for a tithe, the 10 percent offering to God from one's bounty. But the authors rejected the "lesser" tithe because it was without biblical warrant and was unjust. The peasants called for an end to serfdom because it was unjust and unbiblical. Next, they called for the freedom to gather wood in the forests, fish from the streams, and the restitution of communal land. The compilers of the *Articles* supported each of these demands with biblical warrant. For example, they supported the freedom to fish with the Genesis account in which God gives all humans, not just some, dominion over creation. The final demand—that they be judged in all that they said and did by the Bible—conjures up images of Luther's stand at Worms. If the authors of the *Articles* could be shown by Scripture that they were wrong, they would recant.

The *Twelve Articles* provided the people with a standard around which to rally. In a brief period, some 25 editions and approximately 25,000 copies "blanketed the empire."[8] The *Twelve Articles* became the "conceptual glue" that gave the movement form and substance.[9] It combined the peasants' desire for church reform with their need for economic justice in ways that made it easily understood and quickly popular.

As the spring of 1525 dawned, the movement spread to encompass most of Franconia and Thuringia and was beginning to spread into Hesse and Saxony. In Thuringia the expanding peasant revolt met up with the itinerant preacher and scholar Thomas Müntzer.

Thuringia is in central Germany, just northeast of Franconia. Thomas Müntzer was connected to the region through the city of Mühlhausen. An Imperial City, Mühlhausen was a growing agricultural and trade center. Müntzer arrived there in August 1524 as a replacement for priests who chose to leave the city after the success of Henry Pfeiffer in "reforming" the city's churches.[10] By all accounts, Pfeiffer welcomed Müntzer, and each seemed to find in the other a comrade-in-arms. Aware of Müntzer's reputation, however, the Mühlhausen city council sought Luther's opinion of its new preacher. Luther's reply was less than enthusiastic. He warned the council against its new "false prophet."

Luther's warning was too late. Müntzer already had convinced the town of the need for a new civil government. On September 19, 1524, Müntzer and Pfeiffer presented 11 demands to the town council. The *Eleven Mühlhausen Articles* "demanded that government should rest on the Word of God and divine justice, and called for the creation of an 'eternal council' to rule the town under communal control."[11] It was a putsch aimed at theocratic rule. Pfeiffer and Müntzer failed.

By the time the meeting was called, a few of the city councillors had looked for and found support in the surrounding area. On September 27, 1524, Pfeiffer and Müntzer were banished. Müntzer went south to Nuremberg. From there he roamed around Franconia, the Upper Rhine, and eventually Switzerland. This wandering coincided almost perfectly with the roaming peasants' rebellions. In their rebellions, Müntzer saw God at work. He was encouraged and emboldened.

By Christmas 1524, the town council in Mühlhausen had changed enough for Pfeiffer to secure his reinstatement as pastor. By February 1525, the situation had changed enough for Müntzer to return. By the middle of March, Pfeiffer and other prominent Mühlhausen citizens had prevailed in their restructuring of the city council. Energized by the suc-

cess in Mühlhausen, Müntzer quickly began to organize the Eternal
League of God to further the cause. The Eternal League was a military
alliance through which Müntzer planned to spread his reforms. If necessary, he would use force.

The Saxon court remained in a quandary about how to respond to the
situation in Mühlhausen in general and to Müntzer specifically. Only
Duke George of Albertine Saxony and Albrecht, archbishop of Mainz,
openly condemned the renovations in Mühlhausen. The Elector Frederick
was, it seems, too ill to undertake a full examination of the issues confronting him in Mühlhausen and left the situation to God's will.[12] Luther,
however, did not shrink from making his own evaluation. He felt that
Müntzer was establishing a theocracy in Mühlhausen and was preparing to spread that rule elsewhere. In a letter to Nikolaus von Amsdorf in
Magdeburg, Luther refers to Müntzer as the "king and emperor of
Mühlhausen."[13]

When the Peasants' War reached Mühlhausen, its "king and emperor"
was prepared. By that time Müntzer had organized his Eternal League and
had enlisted approximately 600 men. He also had created a standard to
rally around—a flag with a rainbow (a symbol of God's protection) and the
phrase "The Word of God endures forever."

The first campaign of the Eternal League was a great disappointment.
The league's troops marched to the nearby city of Langensalza, but by the
time they arrived, the city and the peasants already had reached an accord.
Disappointed, the troops marched back to Mühlhausen. Along the way
they sacked monasteries, a few churches, and some other property.

Müntzer continued his campaign and next turned his attention to
Alstedt, the city where he had once been pastor. There he encouraged
miners and others to join his glorious cause:

> Go to it, go to it, go to it! The time has come, the evil-doers are run-
> ning like scared dogs! . . . Pay no attention to the cries of the godless.
> They will entreat you ever so warmly, they will whimper and wheedle
> like children. Show no pity, as God has commanded in Deuteronomy
> 7;[14] and he has revealed the same thing to us. . . . The peasants of
> Eichsfeld have commenced action against their Junkers; in brief they
> want no favors from them. There are many similar happenings to
> show you the way. You must go to it, go to it, go to it! The time has
> come. . . . Go to it, go to it, go to it, while the fire is hot! Don't let
> your sword grow cold, don't let it hand down limply! Hammer away
> ding-dong on the anvils of Nimrod, cast down their tower to the

ground! . . . Go to it, go to it, go to it, while it is day! God goes before you follow, follow.[15]

Müntzer signed the letter: "Thomas Müntzer, a servant of God against the godless." The people of Alstedt and Mansfeld heeded his call and went out into the countryside to lay siege to monasteries, abbeys, and castles.

This destruction of church property, government buildings, and public lands led Luther to abandon his previous attempts at a peaceful solution to the growing rebellion. Earlier in the month, on April 15, 1525, Luther had written his *Admonition to Peace*. In that treatise, he addressed the demands of the peasants and set the blame for the present situation at the feet of the lords who did not administer their lands with justice. Luther sought some middle ground in the hope of reconciliation.

As events at Alstedt and Mansfeld demonstrated, by late April the situation in Thuringia had degenerated significantly. Luther felt that the sacking of noncombatant dwellings belied the peasants' assertion in the *Twelve Articles* that they sought only peace. With his customary verve, in the first week of May, Luther delivered a blistering attack on the actions of the peasants. He still felt that the peasants had just grievances; however, their anarchical actions undermined their cause. He called on the lords and princes to put down the rebellion, otherwise disorder and chaos would reign.[16]

Combined with reports from local authorities, Luther's letters finally spurred the princes to action. Following his brother's death, Duke John, now the Elector of Saxony, joined Dukes George of Saxony and Philip of Hesse in the Swabian League to march against the peasants in Thuringia. Müntzer, meanwhile, continued his campaign. In late April, Müntzer promised the city of Frankenhausen (which had written requesting 200 men for support) that "everyone, everyone, as many as we have, wants to come to you, marching through all the countryside and on the way placing ourselves at your disposal."[17] That Müntzer saw God at work in his campaign and that he believed he was motivated by zeal for the Lord are obvious in the signature to the letter: "The community of Christians in the field at Mühlhausen." The language has the ring of "warrior glory." Müntzer is not in Mühlhausen; instead, he is "in the field" with his army at Mühlhausen.[18] Many of these events of late April and early May encouraged Müntzer. In this period the peasant forces met little, if any, resistance. Towns, castles, and lords were forced to surrender. The movement was gaining momentum.

By May 12, 1524, Müntzer was prepared to confront Count Ernst of Mansfeld directly. By this time Müntzer had given up the appellation "servant of God against the godless." Instead, he became the "sword of Gideon," the Old Testament judge whom God used to punish the Midianites.[19] Müntzer now saw himself as God's avenging angel. He wrote to the count, asking him to recant of his sinful attack on the peasants and their cause. He threatened Ernst that if the count failed to repent, Müntzer would march against him and:

> Then you will be hunted down and wiped out. . . . If you will not humble yourself before those of little repute you will be forever disregarded in the sight of the whole Christian people and will become a martyr to the Devil. . . . The eternal, living God has commanded that you should be forcibly cast down from your seat. . . . We want your answer this very evening; otherwise we will descend on you in the name of God of hosts; so you know what to expect. We shall execute without delay what God has commanded us; so do your best, too. I'm on my way![20]

Müntzer set out from Mühlhausen to engage Ernst of Mansfeld at Frankenhausen, where Ernst already had joined forces with Philip of Hesse. Yet Pfeiffer and the vast majority of the Mühlhausen peasants did not join Müntzer. Reports of Philip of Hesse's movements with regular soldiers had already reached Mühlhausen. In an ironic twist, the number of men that did join Müntzer was 300. The number may well have only added to his conviction that he was marching, based on Judg 7:7, to glory.[21] In fact, however, Müntzer was marching toward disaster.

Müntzer arrived in Frankenhausen to a glorious welcome. At about the same time, Albrecht of Mansfeld sought a peaceful solution to the conflagration. Unfortunately, Albrecht seems to have included an admonition to the peasants to cease their destructive behavior by quoting Paul in Romans 2.[22] This did not amuse Müntzer at all! He responded with righteous anger:

> Your quite awful misuse of the epistle of Paul distresses me. . . . Under the name of Christ you want to act the pagan and to use Paul as a cover-up. But your way will be blocked, you can be sure of that! If you will admit, Daniel 7,[23] that God has given power to the common man, and appear before us to give an account of your faith, we will be glad to permit this and to regard you as our common brother. But, if not, then we will not give the least heed to your lame, limp antics but will

fight against you as an arch-enemy of the Christian faith. So, you know what to expect![24]

As though to reinforce his message, he had three of Albrecht's spies executed.

Then Müntzer began to preach. Hans Hut, a man present in Frankenhausen, later recalled the content of the reformer's preaching:

> Müntzer preached publicly in Frankenhausen: the Lord God Almighty would now purify the world; he had taken power from the rulers and given it to their subjects, whereupon the rulers would tremble. In their infirmity the rulers would beg for mercy, but they should not be trusted for they would not keep faith with [their subjects.]

Whatever doubts Müntzer may have had about his course of action vanished when in the midst of one of his sermons someone noticed a rainbow around the sun:

> God was on the subjects' side, for the peasants had painted a rainbow on every banner which they displayed. . . . After three days' preaching to that effect, a rainbow appeared in the sky around the sun. Müntzer pointed to the rainbow, declaring to the peasants: "You see now the rainbow, the league, the sign that God is on your side. You must fight valiantly and be bold!"[25]

Following Müntzer's sermon, his followers began to sing together the hymn "Veni Sancte Spiritus" ("Come, Holy Spirit"). As they were singing, the first barrage of the duke's artillery struck their barricades.[26] The battle of Frankenhausen was over before it started. The peasants were surrounded on all sides. Count Philip von Solms recorded the events of the day in a letter to his son:

> We brought our guns up the slope so that they could fire into [the peasants], and attacked the nearest of them with horse and foot. They did not hold firm, but ran to seek the safety of the town. We gave pursuit and killed the majority of them between the hill and the town, but many got inside. We began to storm the town at once and conquered it speedily, and killed everyone caught there.[27]

A rout was on, and slaughter was the order of the day. By the end of the battle, nearly 6,000 peasants were killed, but only six of the princes' soldiers were wounded. In all, the Peasants' War was devastating for peasants. Contemporary estimates put the total killed in the war at 100,000. Yet

Müntzer survived the day, apparently one of the men who made it into the city during the rout. He was found in bed, feigning ignorance of the day's events and claiming to be ill. Müntzer was arrested and tortured; he confessed, then recanted, and was turned over to Ernst of Mansfeld.

On May 25, 1525, Thomas Müntzer was beheaded at Mühlhausen for treason. His head was placed on a pike as a warning to others. How did a man who began his career as a chaplain in a nunnery end up as the "sword of Gideon"? Müntzer's understanding of Christian identity provides a sharp contrast to Luther's position.

THOMAS MÜNTZER AND CHRISTIAN IDENTITY

Little is known about Müntzer's date of birth, childhood, or family.[28] His family name and his ability to make less than normal pay throughout his career point to his family's minor affluence. In 1506 he entered the University of Leipzig. He also studied at Frankfurt *an der Oder* and eventually arrived in Wittenberg. Müntzer may have been influenced by Luther's reforms, but more likely he came to his convictions about reform before his encounter with Luther. Overall, however, Luther and Müntzer had differing opinions on the type of reform needed. Müntzer agreed with Luther's critique of the papacy. His reflections on martyrdom and the costly nature of grace may also have led Müntzer to support some of Luther's *theologia crucis*. However, while Luther was searching for a gracious God, Müntzer was searching for God's truth.[29]

For Müntzer, God's truth is made known to humankind through the power of the Holy Spirit. Müntzer's theology is an interesting mix of experiential-expressivism and cognitive-propositionalism.[30] In the experiential-expressivist model, knowledge of God is internal and self-referencing. Unlike Luther, who believed the external Word of God confronts the individual and makes demands, Müntzer believed the Holy Spirit reveals the truth inwardly. Müntzer acknowledged that God's call and special revelation were given specifically to him, as God had earlier called Gideon. But that revelation must be shared with the elect. Where Müntzer parted company with many other experiential theologians was in his conviction that the message must be accepted by those to whom he preached. Otherwise hearers separate themselves from the revelation of God and become enemies of Müntzer and of God.

Here Müntzer made the leap from inward experience to ontological reification; he combined experiential-expressivism with propositionalism. In the cognitive-propositionalist model, doctrine or belief "function as informative propositions or truth claims about objective realities."[31] Müntzer combined the two in his understanding of Christian identity. The external world must conform to the objective realities revealed to him through the internal working of the Holy Spirit.

The doctrine of election, therefore, is the driving force behind Müntzer's theology and praxis. God made a covenant with Abraham, instantiated that covenant in the Law given to Moses, and confirmed and expanded that covenant in the life, death, and resurrection of Jesus Christ. That covenant is established in the elect through the witness and power of the Holy Spirit.[32] In other words, God has elected to be our God and that we will be his people.

Christian identity seen through the lens of election plays a significant role in Müntzer's understanding of the relationship of the church to the state. For Müntzer the pastor functions as a teacher and prophet to the state. The pastor does this by seeking to embody his preaching in ordinances (as was done in Mühlhausen) and through implementing his pattern of reform in churches.

Müntzer's active participation in the political process marks a change from that of Luther. Luther involved himself in political questions only reluctantly and only to the degree of stating whether or not a position was sinful.[33] Müntzer's active participation in the political arena reflected his understanding of the church's didactic and prophetic role. In fact, a major portion of his ministry was dedicated to prophetic witness to the rulers of the age. The world must be conformed to the witness of God; the easiest and best way to achieve this goal is through the power and influence of secular rulers. In his *Princes' Sermon*, Müntzer discussed the right relationship of the state to the elect:

> Now if you are to be true rulers you must seize the very roots of government following the command of Christ. St. Paul thinks the same, when he says of the sword that it is set in the hands of the rulers to exact vengeance on the evil and give protection to the good, Romans 13.[34]

Müntzer advocated a state structure that conforms itself to the Word of God and enforces capitulation by the people to that Word as interpreted by Müntzer. The state provides a public manifestation of religion. This is, of course, in keeping with his overall motif of election. The state, too, must conform itself to the Gospel because it also represents God's action in the world. It is also bound by God's covenantal relationship with humanity.

This approach marked a significant departure from Luther. Whereas Luther attempted to distinguish church from state, Müntzer agitated for the community to embody the doctrine of election by patterning its political life after biblical norms. For Müntzer, those who rejected this concept of the kingdom of God belong to the kingdom of Satan:

> But what is one to do with the sword? Exactly this: sweep aside those evil men who obstruct the Gospel! Take them out of circulation! Otherwise you will be Devils not the servants of God which Paul calls you to be in Romans 13. . . . Drive his enemies away from the elect; you are the instruments to do this. My friend, don't let us have any of these hackneyed posturings about the power of God achieving everything without any resort to your sword; otherwise it may rust in its scabbard. . . . Christ speaks clearly enough in Matthew 7, John 15[35] . . . do not therefore, allow the evil-doers, who turns us away from God to continue living, Deut. 13,[36] for a godless man has no right to live if he is hindering the pious. In Exodus 22 God says, "you shall not let the evil-doer live."[37]

The two kingdoms collapse into one.

Müntzer rewrote the medieval concept of the *corpus christianum* into Protestant theology. He changed the locus of legitimization from the Word of God as interpreted by the pope to the witness of the Spirit as interpreted by himself. As Luther noted, the danger for theocracy within Müntzer was powerful.

For Müntzer, the secular ruler must remain in harmony with God's prophetic Word. When rulers no longer embody that prophetic word, they have—as it were—lost their "divine right."

> Hence the sword, too, is necessary to eliminate the godless, Romans 13.[38] To ensure, however, that this now proceeds in a fair and orderly manner, our revered fathers, the princes, who with us confess Christ should carry it out. But if they do not carry it out, the sword will be taken away from them, Daniel 7[39] for then they would confess him in words but deny him in deeds.[40]

The aberrant ruler is like Saul who has been set aside in favor of David.

In such a case, Müntzer advocated the forceful removal of the offending magistrate. His letter to Count Ernst of Mansfeld at Frankenhausen is one example of his advocacy of both resistance to the unlawful intrusion of an unjust ruler and the forceful overthrow of errant rulers.

Müntzer's approval of rebellion is strongly connected to his understanding of Christian identity, that is, election and covenant. To be pious, to be counted among the elect, Christians must overthrow rulers who have abrogated their covenantal responsibilities and roles. The Christian must conform to the Gospel and resist the violating ruler as though he were Satan and, therefore, help reestablish the right ordering of human life.

It is ironic that Müntzer came to be seen as a hero of the masses. But it was not the dream of a proletarian paradise that drew Müntzer to the peasants, it was his theology of election. Had the princes heeded his call to enforce reform, he would never have identified himself with the peasants. Only after the princes rejected him did Müntzer turn to the peasants for help. In turning to the peasants, he also transformed himself from a Daniel-type figure bringing a prophetic word to authority to an avenging angel of God's harsh judgment.

The peasants sought social justice and a revision of laws to better their station in life. Müntzer sought to punish the rulers and establish the kingdom of God. The desires of the former and the latter coalesced only to the degree that the subject of their animosity was the same. Otherwise, their aims had little in common. Müntzer used the common man to further his theological and political agenda.

MARTIN LUTHER AND THE AUGSBURG RECESS

The close connection between Calvinist theology and emancipatory political theory has been amply demonstrated over the years.[41] The connection between Luther and theories of resistance, however, is more tenuous. Uwe Siemon-Netto has demonstrated that it is historically naive to adopt the so-called Shirer thesis.[42] Yet is it possible to find in Luther a *positive* position that influenced thought on resistance to unjust authority?

One starting point is the treatise *Dr. Martin Luther's Warning to His Dear German People*. A draft of the *Warning* was most likely written in October 1530, though it was not published until April 1531.[43] The immediate backdrop for the *Warning* was the collapse of the Diet of Augsburg. The diet began on June 20, 1530. Before and during the diet, Philipp Melanchthon had written a *Confession*[44] summarizing the evangelical position. Melanchthon's tenor at the diet was conciliatory, and he had a "far-reaching desire for peace."[45] This desire for peace by the evangelicals and the lack of such a desire on the part of the Roman delegation was important to Luther, and he makes a great deal of this fact in his *Warning*.

The Roman delegation drafted a *Confutation* to Melanchthon's *Confession*. The unwillingness of the Catholic theologians to give a copy of the *Confutation* to the evangelical delegation confirmed Luther's suspicions regarding the Catholics' agenda. Because of this impasse, the entire diet soon disbanded without agreement, which, for all practical purposes, reinstated the Edict of Worms. Yet the Augsburg Recess itself was more threatening than the Edict of Worms because it allowed for legal prosecution of the evangelicals, making provisions for the Imperial Supreme Court to try any who did not capitulate to the *Confutation*'s demands. This was a real and substantial, if unlikely, threat.

Fortunately, the emperor's continuing problems maintaining the integrity of his borders lessened the threat. In the early 1530s, continuing skirmishes with the Turks to his south plagued Charles V. In late 1530, the scene looked particularly ominous, and the Protestants did not feel secure. One indication of their insecurity was Elector John of Saxony's proposal for a defensive league, which he put forth the day after the draft of the Recess was read. The anxiety is also palpable in Luther's *Warning*. Both expressed a genuine fear that the emperor would march against the Protestants. The princes decided that they would resist an attack and looked to the theologians for biblical support.

To that end, the theologians were summoned to Torgau in October to discuss with the princes' legal scholars the matter of the right of resistance. Following the Torgau meeting, where the lawyers made a strong case for the legality of resistance based in positive law, the theologians took a position of "guarded neutrality" concerning the lawyers' position.[46] Although the theologians were willing to grant the argument that princes might have a legal right to resistance, they were, however, unwilling to move beyond that position. Their position was summarized in the famous *Torgau Declaration*, issued in late October 1530 by Luther, Jonas, Melanchthon, Spalatin, and other theologians. It stated:

> We are in receipt of a memorandum from which we learn that the doctors of law have come to an agreement on the question: In what situations may one resist the government? Since this possibility has now been established by these doctors and experts in the law, and since we certainly are in the kind of situation in which, as they show, resistance to the government is permissible, and since, further, we have always taught that one should acknowledge civil laws, submit to them, and respect their authority, inasmuch as the Gospel does not militate against civil laws, we cannot invalidate from Scripture the right of men to defend themselves even against the emperor in person, or anyone acting in his name. And now that the situation everywhere has become so dangerous that events may daily make it necessary for men to take immediate measure to protect themselves, not

only on the basis of civil law but on the grounds of duty and distress of conscience, it is fitting for them to arm themselves and to be prepared to defend themselves against the use of force; and such may easily occur, to judge by the present pattern and course of events. For in previously teaching that resistance to governmental authorities is altogether forbidden, we were unaware that this right has been granted by the government's own laws which we have diligently taught are to be obeyed at all times.[47]

In fact, the reformers were "caught" in Luther's own doctrine of the two kingdoms. As Christians, people may not resist the authorities put above them by God, but as "political-individuals" they are "obligated to obey positive law, even if that obedience led to active resistance to the emperor."[48]

Following this meeting, the Landgrave Philip of Hesse, the major advocate of the right to resistance, asked Luther to write a treatise for popular consumption on what had been discussed at Torgau. Luther responded with his *Warning*. According to some scholars, this treatise must have greatly disappointed the Landgrave: "The *Warnung an seine lieben Deutschen* was not . . . quite what Philip had in mind. In it Luther specifically disclaimed the intent to summon anyone to resistance."[49] W. D. J. Cargill Thompson suggests that Luther's position in the *Warning* is equivocal and ambiguous.[50] But while the treatise may at times be ambiguous, it is never equivocal. Often Luther couches his arguments in carefully worded caveats;[51] these caveats ring hollow, however, when they are placed next to the tremendous vigor with which he defends those who oppose the papists.

The *Warning* was most likely everything the Landgrave wanted and more.[52] Mark Edwards correctly perceives Luther's emotional and moral outrage in the document.

> What explains Luther's righteous anger? Luther himself gives us a key in the *Warning*. The intransigence of the Roman delegation at Augsburg and the harshness of the Recess convinced Luther that reconciliation with the papists was now hopeless. Luther and his colleagues sought reconciliation and indeed prayed for those who opposed them; however, the recent actions betray the fact that: God is demonstrating mightily that he does not want to hear our intercession in their behalf, but he is letting them go and sin against the Holy Spirit, as Pharaoh did, until they are beyond hope of repentance and reform.[53]

Luther was convinced that God had hardened the hearts of the Roman theologians and delegates. This intransigence prompted him to write and publish his *Warning*. Edwards posits two functions to the *Warning*: to strengthen the resolve to resist and to ease the consciences of those who resist.[54] A third function was to warn those who would side with the emperor that they would risk their immortal souls.

The *Warning* is divided into three sections: first, a survey of the situation; second, the apology for resistance; and finally, the warning. The first two sections are addressed primarily to evangelicals; the third section is addressed to those who would side with the emperor.

A survey of Luther's opinion of the Diet of Augsburg begins the first section. He expresses concern that God has hardened the hearts of the papists and that, like the Pharaoh, the papists depend not on God, but on force. He asserts that the evangelicals had made repeated efforts to achieve unity and reconciliation, but the papists, not the evangelicals, are fostering rebellion.[55] Luther concludes this section by expressing his confidence that the papists, because they oppose the Gospel, will ultimately fail.[56]

Luther moves in the second section to an apology for resistance. He builds the groundwork for the first two aspects of a resistance theory. In the first argument for a right to resist (that within positive law a right of resistance exists), he refers those who have questions to the Hessian and Saxon jurists who had earlier convinced Luther of the legality—if not the sinlessness—of resistance. Then he proceeds to natural law, of which a primary element is the right to self-defense. Luther condemns the assumption on the part of the Roman theologians that resistance is *rebellion*; it is, in fact, *self-defense*. Luther writes, "Furthermore, if war breaks out—which God forbid—I will not reprove those who defend themselves against the murderous and bloodthirsty papists, nor let anyone else rebuke them as being seditious."[57]

For Luther, resistance in this case is not rebellion because the Protestants have continually sought peace; the Roman delegates are the peace-breakers and, therefore, the rebellion-makers. Moreover, a position cannot be condemned without a fair hearing. To Luther the actions of the Roman delegation at Augsburg demonstrated that a fair hearing was not granted. Worse, the evangelical position was never even considered.

The final section is Luther's simple warning to the opponents of reform: Do not side with the emperor or you risk body and soul.[58] Those who oppose the evangelicals risk their souls for four reasons:

1. To oppose reform is to fight against the Gospel.

2. By fighting against reform, one tacitly supports all the abominations of the papacy and takes them on as one's own.[59]

3. If one fights for the emperor, one will overthrow the Gospel and all the good that reform has done.

4. Fighting will help restore the kingdom of the devil.

While Luther's audience here is not the evangelicals, and though the warning functions to justify passive resistance of those who otherwise would fight on the emperor's behalf, the third section bears a clear connection to later resistance theories. In this part of the *Warning*, Luther lays the foundation for what will become the most important argument for the right to resist: The Gospel itself is at stake. The forces arrayed against the Protestants are none other than the legions of the antichrist poised to reinstate the dominion of Satan. A tyrant who attacks the proclamation of the Gospel and thus sides with Satan must be resisted. Later advocates of resistance, most notably the Magdeburg pastors and Theodore Beza, took this admonition and applied it to their situations.

CONCLUSION

Luther is often accused of engendering political quietism. Careful exegesis of Luther's *Warning* refutes that position. Yet to appreciate Luther's understanding of the Christian and the right of believers to resist, one must first understand the historical context of the various positions and practices.

For Thomas Müntzer, the Bible is a social blueprint for how a just society ought to be organized and governed. For Luther, using the Bible for building a society is a quixotic dream. Instead, Luther argued that reason ought to guide the state in its action.

The most fundamental implication of Müntzer's theory, as compared with Luther's, is the starting point for rebellion or resistance. From Müntzer's position, one can rebel at the point where a ruler begins to abrogate his covenantal responsibilities as outlined in Scripture. To put government back "on the right track," the people must rebel. Therefore, to resist is not sinful; rather, it is, of its essence, conforming to the Gospel.

Luther joins the fray later because for him the locus of authority in government is not the Word of God, but reason. History is also more veiled for Luther, akin to his understanding of *Deus absconditus*. The question of resistance is always a question of conscience for Luther. Because the Christian cannot state with certainty where God is and where he is not in the political realm, any decision about where God is acting in the state is sinful. It is sinful because a person is attempting to answer a question that only God can decide. If humanity could not recognize Christ on the cross, how can it be trusted to recognize a righteous king?

The difficulty for resistance is that one must make such a decision. If one is going to resist, that person must decide that the king is not acting as an agent of God. Luther casts the question of resistance on the Christian conscience. Because this decision impinges on God's domain, however, it is always to be regarded as a sinful act.

From Müntzer's position, Luther's view on the sinful quality of resistance would engender a general hesitancy toward resistance. This turns Luther into a "flatterer of the Princes," "Father Pussyfoot," "Brother Soft-Life," "Malicious Raven," "Doctor Liar," etc.[60] If resistance to the state is sinful, then co-option is the only option.

However, Luther was unwilling to give secular authority carte blanche. When a ruler attacks the proclamation of the Gospel—by inference, attacks the Gospel itself—then he betrays his allegiance and is, in Luther's words, a "werewolf"[61] who must be resisted.

Even when one deals with a "werewolf," the resistance is still sinful. The assurance that one has made a proper decision *coram deo* is, of course, impossible because one can never view a situation from God's perspective. Nevertheless, in keeping with Luther's admonition to live in faith, the Christian must sin boldly and resist.[62]

Yet Luther's view that it is legitimate to resist the civil authorities when they oppose the Gospel differs from the situation behind the Peasants' War. In seeking religious legitimization for his revolution, Müntzer confused the lines between the spiritual and secular realms. Luther's position was that the peasants should have sought their goals on the basis of justice (the Law) in the political realm rather than in the realm of the Gospel. He wrote:

> Your name and title ought therefore to indicate that you are people who fight because they will not and ought not endure injustice or evil according to the teaching of nature. You should use that name and let the name of Christ alone, for that is the kind of works you are doing.

The peasants' calls for reform were, in fact, legitimate. The problem was in mixing one's justifiable claims in the political realm with the Gospel. Luther continued:

> If, however, you will not take that name, but keep the name of Christian, then I must accept the fact that I am also involved in this struggle and consider you as enemies who, under the name of the Gospel act contrary to it and want to do more to suppress my Gospel than anything the pope and the emperor have done to suppress it.[63]

For Luther, "the identification of any political program, regardless of its intrinsic merit, with the will of God is to subvert both politics and the Gospel."[64]

On the other hand, Müntzer believed that the Christian in good conscience could and should use the political process to achieve the objectives of the church. Although the Peasants' War would have happened without Müntzer, his participation gave the people theological as well as social justification for their action, thus feeding the flames of rebellion.

In collapsing the two kingdoms, Müntzer removed a necessary check and balance on resistance. He equated his political program with God's activity of redemption. One who followed Müntzer's system was called on to decide where God is at work. The person who sided with Müntzer was saved; the one who decided against him was damned and damnable. Given his assurance of the inward revelation of the Spirit, that distinction may have been easy for Müntzer. But how can such a system be expanded to create a legacy to be adopted by others?

For Luther, Müntzer's political theology suffered from the fundamental flaw of all utopian ideologies: the belief that salvation can be achieved rather than received. This perspective regards righteousness *coram deo* as dependent on righteousness *coram hominibus*. It drove Müntzer to see in current political situations divine implications. It led him to rebel against the rulers of his age and resulted in the slaughter of his people.

Luther thought that the situation in 1531 was markedly different from the one in 1525. In 1525 Müntzer used the Gospel to "baptize" a political agenda; in 1531 Luther felt the Gospel itself was under attack. Yet an important question must be addressed: Did Luther abandon some of his fundamental beliefs to accept resistance? Was he, therefore, more dedicated to the political survival of his reforms than he was to his previous positions? Was his position in 1531 merely a function of the fact that he, instead of Müntzer, was now being confronted, an intellectually expedient maneuver used to justify a necessary course of action that would have been undertaken regardless? Cynthia Shoenberger has written

> To conclude then: having started from a position of complete opposition to resistance of any kind, Luther came eventually to embrace a

notion of resistance . . . Certainly forcible resistance was meant to be a last resort and even then to be exercised in a carefully circumscribed manner; but it is significant that each time his church was in peril during the 1530s and 1540s, Luther did on one or another ground allow the possibility of resistance.[65]

This issue is substantial and important because it goes to the heart of Luther's convictions about peace, justice, order, obedience, and, ultimately, about his self-understanding as a preacher. The issue is not, however, new. Luther himself was confronted with this allegation when, soon after the publication of his *Warning*, he received a letter from Lazarus Spengler, chancellor of Nuremberg. Spengler was concerned that Luther had abandoned his position on obedience to the emperor. In responding to Spengler, Luther assured him of three things. First, his primary concern is to ensure that the Gospel can be preached. Second, he has not abandoned the fundamental position that authority ought to be obeyed. Third, he has, though, been persuaded that the emperor has (through his own laws) allowed for resistance.

In his response, Luther made several important points. First, the primary concern of Luther and the princes who supported him was the preservation of the Gospel. They took seriously the threat of the Recess and its implications not just for themselves, but also for the proclamation of the Gospel. Second, though Luther modified his position in light of the changing political situation, nevertheless he remained committed to his fundamental principles.

The first principle that Luther outlined, and which he consistently followed throughout his life, was the fundamental position that authority ought to be obeyed. This was a principle that the Magdeburg pastors also adopted. Yet obedience is never to be blind obedience; it has limits.[66] In his many letters to the Elector Frederick, to Charles V, and to the pope, Luther made this position clear: He is willing to be obedient. However, he could not and would not recant unless he can be shown his error on the basis of Scripture.[67] God must be obeyed before men.[68] Throughout his career, Luther consistently adhered to this principle.

Second, Luther remained consistent in his position that the realms of God's creation—the secular and the spiritual—must not be confused. Luther did not, contrary to Cargill Thompson, abdicate his responsibility when he deferred to the jurists on issues of the legality of resistance.[69] Luther could not have interfered in the legal realm on the basis of the Gospel without violating his own two kingdoms doctrine.

A serious and important implication of this doctrine was that each kingdom was freed from the undue influence of the other. Based on his Law/Gospel dialectic, Luther also maintained that a person should act within one's area of competency. His own area of competency was the Bible, not the laws of the empire. For Luther to interfere in imperial affairs would have been improper. True, Luther could preach (and often did) on political affairs, but he spoke on the basis of the Gospel. The Gospel cannot proclaim what is legal, only what God has accomplished and revealed in Christ.[70] The freedom of the secular realm from ideological servitude to the spiritual realm (and vice versa) was an important, consistent tenet in Luther's thought.

Third, Luther consistently believed and taught that religion cannot be established by force. To seek to do so would corrupt both the Law and the Gospel. This position is clearly evident in Luther's early public writings (e.g., *Invocavit Sermons*), but he also made the point in private correspondence. For example, when it seemed as though the emperor might demand that Frederick turn Luther over to him, Luther wrote to Frederick, "If I thought that Your Electoral Grace could and would protect me, I should not go. The sword ought not, and cannot, help a matter of this kind."[71]

The caricatures of Luther as a lackey of the princes or as one who adopted politically expedient positions and of Müntzer as a proletarian hero are grossly misleading. Luther remained consistent in his convictions about the Gospel and its proclamation. Both Luther and Müntzer advocated theological theories of resistance. The difference between them was not only in their outcomes, but also in their fundamental understandings of what it means to be a Christian—Christian identity—and for human beings to relate properly to God.

In the next chapter, we will examine another early conflict between the church and the state that involved the Magdeburg pastors. In this conflict, the pastors often advocated positions similar to those of Müntzer, but they claimed Luther as their theological father. Whose legacy did they best represent?

The Context
of *The Magdeburg Confession*

Rulers are not a terror to good conduct, but to bad. (Romans 13:3)

Alas for you, what is this we hear? Are not the people, of themselves sheep without a pastor? If the magistrates and other officers condemn their duty in defending God's glory and the Laws committed to their charge, does it not lie in our power to remedy it? Shall we that are subjects take the sword in our hands? It is indeed as you say, a great discouragement to the people when they are not stirred up to godliness by the good example of all sorts of superiors, magistrates and officers in the faithful executing of their office: and so much more when they are not defended by them in their right and title, as well concerning religion, as the freedom of their natural country: but most of all when they, which should be their guides and captains, have become instruments to enforce them to wicked impiety.—Christopher Goodman, *How Superior Magistrates Ought To Be Obeyed By Their Subjects*

Introduction

Christopher Goodman's *How Superior Powers Ought To Be Obeyed By Their Subjects: And Wherein They May Lawfully By God's Word Be Disobeyed And Resisted* was published in Geneva in 1558. Goodman claimed that Calvin had read the document and completely supported its contents. The work was well-known during the 16th and 17th centuries and went farther than any previous Reformation writing on resistance when it claimed that not only did lesser magistrates have the authority—even the duty—to resist, but so did the common people. This aspect of Goodman's work made him influential and a popular author with other leading advocates of resistance, including John Knox, John Locke, and Thomas Jefferson. Because of

Goodman, Knox, and Locke, Calvinism is identified in popular opinion with the rise of democracy and the resistance of tyranny.

Perhaps more than any other thinker in the Reformed tradition, however, Theodore Beza, John Calvin's associate and later successor as head of the Venerable Pastors in Geneva, was most responsible for Calvinist understandings of resistance. In 1554, Beza published a short treatise on secular government.[1] Prompted as a response to the arrest of Michael Servetus, the treatise examines the role of secular authority in general.

Beza's thoughts concerning secular authority largely mirror John Calvin's. David Willis notes that in Calvin's thought the church functions as a teacher and prophet to the state. The church does this by seeking to embody its preaching in ordinances (as was done in Geneva) and through the synod system.[2] Calvin himself personified this relationship excellently. While Calvin had no real juridical power in Geneva (much less, in fact, than the previous bishop), his *de facto* power in the city-state was more significant and far-reaching.[3]

Calvin's active participation in the political arena reflected his understanding of the church's didactic and prophetic—covenantal—role. What role did Calvin understand the state to play? Calvin closed his *Institutes*, written to the king of France as an apologetic, with a discussion of the right relationship of the state to the church:

> [Civil government] prevents idolatry, sacrilege against God's name, blasphemies against his truth, and other public offenses against religion from arising and spreading among the people; it prevents the public peace from being disturbed, it provides that each man may keep his property safe and sound; that men may carry on blameless intercourse among themselves; that honesty and modesty may be preserved among men. In short, *it provides that a public manifestation of religion may exist among Christians*, and that humanity be maintained among men.[4]

It appears that Calvin advocated a state structure that conforms itself to the Word of God. The state provides a "public manifestation of religion." Calvin, himself, was aware of this problem and noted in the next paragraph that no one should be concerned that he has committed to civil government the role of "rightly establishing religion."[5] However, the rhetorical weight of his argument flowed against this caveat in the previous section in which he stated, "[C]ivil government has its appointed end, so long as we live among men, to cherish and protect the outward worship of God, to defend sound doctrine of piety and the position of the church."[6]

Calvin did draw the lines that separate the church from the state very closely. They never touch, and they do not overlap. Nevertheless, when this plays out in life, Calvin's positions strike one as a distinction without a difference. This distinction without a difference raised a significant question in Beza: What if the authority turned from supporting to attacking the right worship of God? Beza writes:

> What then if the Lord grant us princes who either through apparent cruelty or through crass ignorance combat the reign of Christ? First of all the Church should take refuge in prayers and tears, and correct its life. For these are the arms of the faithful for overcoming the rages of the world. However, the inferior magistrate must, as much as possible, with prudence and moderation, yet constantly and wisely, maintain pure religion in the area under his authority. A signal example of this has been shown in our times by Magdeburg, that city on the Elbe . . . When then several Princes abuse their office, whoever still feels it necessary to refuse to use the Christian Magistrates offered by God against external violence whether of the unfaithful or of heretics, I charge deprives the Church of God a most useful and necessary defense.[7]

In this text Beza sets out his understanding of a right to resistance against a tyrannical authority. God has provided the church with a remedy for tyranny—the lesser magistracy.

Christopher Goodman picked up on this theme, as did John Knox. The allusion to Magdeburg is especially significant. From Beza's later writing, *On the Rights of Magistrates*, it is clear that he had in mind *The Magdeburg Confession*. To maintain anonymity, Beza originally published *On the Rights of Magistrates* as a "revision" or "reprint" of that treatise "published by those of Magdeburg in 1550 and now revised and augmented with several reasons and examples."[8]

The connection between *The Magdeburg Confession* and Theodore Beza places the *Confession* at the center of the debate over political resistance in Reformation thought. *The Magdeburg Confession* is, therefore, one of the most important documents of the Reformation on political theology, and it played a key and positive role in the development of resistance theory.

The Magdeburg pastors and churches considered themselves to be Lutherans. They also claimed Luther as their theological father. But are their claims true? They viewed themselves as modern-day Maccabees; is Müntzer, then, a more appropriate theological forefather? Did the authors of *The Magdeburg Confession* blaze a new trail? Or did they continue on one already begun by Luther? Or, while giving lip service to Luther, did they really follow Müntzer? The significant parallels to Luther's treatise on political resistance (*Dr. Martin Luther's Warning to His Dear German People*), his doctrine of the two kingdoms, and his thought on Christian identity make *The Magdeburg Confession* a genuine evangelical Lutheran document. As such, it represents the theological legacy of Luther, not Müntzer.

CONNECTIONS

The authors of the *Confession* held Luther in the highest regard, and his theology served as the document's primary source.[9] One of Luther's closest friends, Nikolaus von Amsdorf, is the first signer. The connection between the *Confession* and Luther's *Warning* is made plain in the preface, where the authors note "anyone may read further about this in the book which Dr. Martin Luther wrote as a warning to his dear Germans."[10] The intention is obvious: The authors do not consider themselves to be writing an original work, but they see themselves as continuing on a path already marked by Luther.

Why did the authors look to Luther and specifically to his *Warning*? The social context of the pastors in Magdeburg was strikingly similar to that of Luther at the time he wrote the *Warning*. Both *The Magdeburg Confession* and the *Warning* are apologies for resistance.

CONTEXT

Luther's fears of an imperial invasion were unfulfilled in his lifetime. Constantly changing conditions seemed to conspire against the emperor. Both the Turks and the French represented severe threats. However, by 1546 the situation was stabilized, and skirmishes on these two fronts lessened considerably. The emperor was now free to turn his attention to the Protestants.

To that end Charles V made overtures to the pope about the possibility of an alliance. A treaty signed on June 7, 1546, confirmed this alliance. With guarantees of financial and troop support from the pope, Charles was prepared to move against the Protestants, charging them with violating imperial law. In a letter to his sister Mary, he disclosed his real intentions:

> If we do not intervene now, all the estates of the Empire, including the Netherlands, would be in danger of abandoning the faith. After I

had considered all this again and again, I decided to start war against Hesse and Saxony as violators of the peace in regard to the Duke of Braunshweig and his territory. And although this pretext will not cover up for long that it is a question of religion, at first anyway it will serve to separate those who have deviated.[11]

The emperor's pretext was indeed short-lived because the Protestants knew immediately what was at stake. This new crisis led Melanchthon to reissue Luther's *Warning*.[12] Luther's fears of a war over religion were now coming to fulfillment. Although Luther had died in February prior to the conclusion of the alliance between the emperor and the pope, his *Warning* was as relevant in 1546 as it has been in 1531.

The war did not go well for the Protestants. After initial stalls, the emperor's forces moved quickly to victory. On May 10, 1547, the Elector John Frederick of Saxony, who had been captured by the imperial forces at the Battle of Mühlberg several weeks before, was condemned to death—a sentence later commuted to imprisonment. (The sentence, however, was never carried out.) The same fate soon befell the Landgrave Philip of Hesse when he surrendered to the emperor on June 19.

The situation solved no problems and only created more strife. Instead of looking to the Council of Trent for the resolution of the Protestant problem, the emperor was forced to seek a "German" solution. That solution was the Diet of Augsburg, which opened on September 1, 1547. Out of this diet came the infamous Augsburg Interim. The Interim reinstated many of the liturgical practices abandoned by the Protestants (e.g., ceremonies and vestments at the Mass and the feast of *Corpus Christi*).[13] To make this accommodation acceptable, the Wittenberg theologians put forward an interpretation of doctrine in which practices neither commanded nor forbidden by Scripture were considered to be *adiaphoristic*, or "indifferent things."

The Interim suffered from a number of structural difficulties. First, it was a theological and liturgical mandate set forth by a victorious army. This provided a ready-made opposition. Second, the claim of *adiaphora* was tenuous at best. Almost immediately a group emerged that opposed the Augsburg Interim. They came to be called Gnesio-Lutherans ("true Lutherans").[14] The Gnesio-Lutherans were led by a young follower of Luther, Matthias Flacius Illyricus, who had left Wittenberg over the imposition of the Interim. He found his way to Magdeburg, but his arrival in Magdeburg was not accidental. Nikolaus von Amsdorf, who headed Magdeburg's churches, had been a close confidant and friend of Luther's and a consistent proponent of resistance.[15] The city itself had a tradition and reputation for resistance that could be traced back to 1325 when citizens rebelled against what they saw as an abuse of power by the city's lord, Archbishop Burkhart III. The citizens murdered him in the Rathaus cellar.[16] The city's acceptance of the Reformation only reinforced this tradition. In the early years of the Reformation, Magdeburg's Archbishop Albert had been a vociferous opponent of Luther's reforms. Despite his political authority as the city's lord and against his wishes, the city adopted the Reformation in 1524 and forced Albert into exile.

In many ways, Magdeburg's ecclesial reforms reinforced its political aspirations. In 1528 the city council refuted the claim that the city belonged to the archbishop. They felt the archbishop had usurped Magdeburg's independent status originally granted by Emperor Otto I in the 10th century. The city had some legitimate claims to the status of a "Free Imperial City." Since the 10th century, for example, the city maintained the rights to a market, to levy taxes, and to mint money.

The advent of the Reformation in Magdeburg served the city's political aspirations well—at least in the beginning. By adopting evangelical theology and practice, the city was able to free itself from the archbishop. Soon after the adoption of the Reformation, the city began referring to itself as *reichsfreie* and *kaiserliche*.[17] It also joined the Schmalkaldic League in 1526, a further effort to demonstrate its freedom.

Despite its pre-Reformation history, Magdeburg was, for all intents and purposes, part of the archbishop's domain. Since the murder of Burkhart, the city councillors had to swear allegiance to the lord archbishop. It is, therefore, of little surprise that the councillors of Magdeburg would find in the Reformation an opportunity to overthrow or oust an unwanted authority. Yet throughout this ordeal with the emperor, the first and primary concern was the preservation of evangelical preaching.[18] To its critics, the city's adherence to the Reformation was merely an expedient means to ensure its political autonomy. But this view must be rejected for a number of reasons. First, in siding with the Reformation in the Schmalkaldic League, Magdeburg lost its "Free Imperial City" privileges. Charles V revoked them and granted them to another city further up the Elbe (Tangermünde). Second, in the late 1540s siding with the Reformation against Charles V was an unpromising avenue to political autonomy. By the time that Magdeburg began to shelter political refugees, Charles V was marching toward almost certain victory; in fact, many of the refugees arriving in Magdeburg came from lands already lost to the emperor. In each and every case, victory by Charles marked a political loss of status—not an increase.[19]

Thus, Magdeburg refused to capitulate to the emperor's demands first and foremost because of her commitment to the Reformation.[20] A consequence of her position was that the city quickly gained a reputation in Germany of heroic resistance to the imposition of "papist heresy." As more political and religious refugees flocked to the city, this influx of "true believers" reinforced the city's conviction that she had chosen the just course and buttressed her resolve against capitulation.

The city attracted men such as Amsdorf, Gallus (who already had a reputation for fierce rhetoric and a willingness to resist), Erasmus Alberus (a harsh critic of the Interim), and Flacius (perhaps the most vehement opponent of the Interim).

More than the others, Flacius used his time in Magdeburg to build support for the city and her cause. During this period, Flacius coined a famous phrase regarding the Interim. He wrote: "*In casu confessionis et scandali nihil est adiaphora*" ("In cases of confession and inducement to sin nothing is indifferent").[21]

Flacius and the other Gnesio-Lutherans considered themselves to be the true protectors of Luther's theology.[22] They set out on a propaganda campaign to win popular support for the cause. They issued hundreds of tracts, pamphlets, and broadsheets. Over time, the propaganda campaign of Magdeburg accounted for "most of the 147 books and pamphlets listed by Hüssle for the siege years of 1550–1551."[23]

The campaign led people throughout Saxony to call Magdeburg "Our Lord's Chancellery." Oliver K. Olson describes the situation of Magdeburg in 1549:

> The tense situation, in which it seemed that Luther's movement was about to be crushed, helped form an ecclesiastical party that in one guise or other has persisted with Lutheran tradition ever since, a party claiming to preserve Luther's true intent. Thus Melanchthon's observation that 'these absurd persons consider themselves the only Gnesio [true] Lutherans' had a kernel of truth. Their convictions were expressed by the soldiers of the city's garrison. Outnumbered six to one, they defended Magdeburg as the Saxon elector, in a mopping-up operation after the Schmalkaldic War, mounted a siege against the city on the emperor's behalf. Under constant fire, they sang about themselves as the last faithful remnant of Luther's cause—modern Maccabees.[24]

Out of this crisis came a theologically justified apology for resistance.

Bekentnis Vnter-
richt vnd vermanung/ der Pfarr-
hern vnd Prediger/ der Christlichen
Kirchen zu Magdeburgk.

Anno 1550. Den 13. Aprilis.

Psalm. 119.

Ich rede von deinen zeugnissen für Königen/ vnd sche-
me mich derselben nicht.

Roma. 13.

Die Gewaltigen sind von Gott nicht den guten wer-
cken/ sondern den bösen zufürchten verordnet.

Acto. 9.

Saul/ Saul/ was verfolgestu MICH? Es wird dir
schwer werden/ wider den stachel lecken.

Cover of *The Magdeburg Confession*.

4

THE MAGDEBURG CONFESSION
OVERVIEW AND INTERPRETATION

Give therefore to the emperor the things that are the emperor's and to God the things that are God's. (Matthew 22:21)

If a government wishes to be Christian and further Christ's kingdom, it may do so as an individual person, but its office remains the same one way or the other. And if it is not proper for Turks and heathen to meddle in Christ's kingdom with the sword, it is even less so for a Christian Government.—Anonymous, *Whether Secular Government Has the Right to Wield the Sword in Matters of Faith* (Nürnberg 1530)

INTRODUCTION

Of the many tracts and treatises published during the defense of Magdeburg,[1] the most complete and influential was the *Confession, Instruction, and Warning of the Pastors and Preachers of the Christian Church in Magdeburg*, which was published in April 1550.[2] Authorship of the document is debated. Some argue that Nikolaus von Amsdorf was the primary author.[3] Oliver K. Olson quotes a handwritten note by Johann Wigand that attributes authorship to Nicholas Gallus, superintendent of Ratisbon.[4] In either scenario, the document clearly represents the theological and philosophical positions of both individuals.

The *Confession* represents the culmination of the Magdeburg pastors' theological reflection on the issues facing the church and city. It is careful in style, grammar, and notation. Like many other church petitions, the *Confession* was addressed primarily to Emperor Charles V.[5] The pastors make clear in the "Introduction" that their intention was to present a complete summary of their thinking and positions on both sacred doctrine and the right to resist. They did not write simply to edify their readers but to reassure the convinced, to persuade the unsure, and to convince the opposed.

The rhetorical character of the writing that pervades the entire document begins already on the title page. Three quotations from Scripture, situated below the title and above the city's coat of arms, set the tone and context for everything that will follow.

The first quotation from Psalm 119[6] provides the pastors' rationale for writing: In the tradition of Nathan preaching to King David,[7] the pastors must speak God's truth to the powerful. The second quotation, from Romans 13, is the most interesting and best discloses the authors' inclinations. It defines the truth they must speak: God commands the powerful to be a terror to evil and not to the good. What makes this quotation interesting is that it is not a direct translation from either the Erasmus edition of the Greek New Testament or a quotation from Luther's German translation.

Erasmus's Greek text reads οἱ γὰρ ἄρχοντες οὐκ εἰσὶν φόβος τῷ ἀγαθὸν ποίει.[8] Luther's translation of that text reads, "Denn die Gewaltigen sind nicht den guten wercken, Sondern den bösen zu fürchten."[9] The pastors had their own translation of the text: "Die Gewaltigen sind von Gott nicht den guten wercken sondern den bösen zufürchten verordnet" ("The powerful are commanded by God to fear not good works but evil ones"). The pastors added three words: *verorden* (to order or command) and *von Gott* (by God). Why? The addition of those three words asserts and supports their cause.

Romans 13 plays an integral role in any discussion of political resistance. The authors of the *Confession* understood this and began here to shape their later examination of the subject. In unambiguous terms, Paul states that resistance to authority is resistance against God. The apostle makes the declarative statement, "rulers are not a terror to good conduct but to bad."[10] However, this simple sentence does not fully deal with the complexities of the current situation in Magdeburg. In the body of the *Confession*, the pastors attempted to demonstrate two things. First, they represent the good, and second, by terrorizing them, the ruler has forsaken his God-given mandate to rule. Their support for this argument began on the title page where they turned Paul's declarative statement into a divine imperative, i.e., *God commands you*. This small but significant revision of the text has major import. If the emperor ignores this divine imperative, he has forsaken his responsibility and nullified his divine mandate. Thus, he may be justly resisted.

Another seemingly minor but important distinction must be made here as well. At first impression, the pastors have more in common with Müntzer than with Luther. The important distinction is between general and special revelation. Müntzer felt that authorities had a divine imperative to *instantiate* the Gospel in civil life and law, that is, to make the Gospel the standard for determining what is legal and illegal, what is encouraged and what is discouraged. The Magdeburg pastors make no such claim. Ruling through law is a part of God's *general* revelation. Pagan kings, too, must punish the wicked. From this perspective, the Magdeburg pastors will judge the actions of the emperor based on the standard of God's general revelation and not in terms of the emperor's consonance with the Gospel.

The final quotation is from Acts[11] and alludes to Saul of Tarsus, the first persecutor of the church. The pastors note that those who persecute the true church are subject to God's judgment. Each of the three quotes sets the tone for the argument put forth in the document.

The *Confession* begins with a one-page "Short Summary of the Contents of this Book," followed by an 11-page "Introduction." The body of the treatise is divided into three sections. The first section (chapters 1–7) recapitulates the main doctrinal *loci* of the *Augsburg Confession*. The second section discusses resistance theory, and the third section provides a warning to those who oppose Magdeburg's actions.

In the first paragraph of the work, the pastors set out what they consider to be the fundamental issue confronting them: the abuse of power by an unjust ruler in the persecution of the church. The only solution: resistance by lesser magistrates. They write:

> If the high authority does not refrain from persecuting with force and injustice not only the persons of their subjects, but even more their rights under Divine and Natural Law, and if the high authority does not desist from suspending or eradicating true doctrine and true worship of God, then the lesser magistracy is required by God's divine injunction to attempt, together with their subjects, to stand up, as far as possible, to such superiors.[12]

In defining this fundamental issue, the pastors outlined the arguments they would later develop in the body of the work to support their contention that resistance to the Interim is just and necessary.

First, the pastors allege that the emperor and his allies, not the citizens of Magdeburg, are disturbing the peace. They argue that they are upright and honest subjects of the empire. They had done nothing illegal or immoral. The insinuation is that the emperor ought to leave them alone and focus his attention on those who, in fact, disturb the public order. The emperor has a God-given duty to carry out this responsibility—he should fulfill his secular duty.[13] In this brief section, the Magdeburg pastors thoroughly integrate Luther's doctrine of the two kingdoms into their thought.

Second, the pastors promise to demonstrate that their beliefs represent true Christian doctrine through "powerful arguments from the Word of God." The Augsburg *Confutation* that the emperor seeks to enforce was written, they maintain, "unskillfully and without any basis in God's Word."[14] This point supports their previous assertion that the emperor is the disturber of the peace and characterizes the pastors' resistance as defensive in nature. The pope's theologians have refuted neither the *Augsburg Confession* nor the Lutheran position from God's Word; instead, they seek to overthrow it by force.

Here again, Luther's doctrine of the two kingdoms is important. The Gospel must be preached and persons convicted by the Word alone. The only appropriate use of the sword is for the maintenance of public order: "it is not appropriate to defend God's Word with force and although it is now happening, this does not turn the truth into lies."[15] By using the sword improperly, the emperor violated the public order; all that the Magdeburg pastors did was to defend themselves against this injustice.

The Magdeburg pastors held that the emperor's actions only served to encourage those who support resistance. They affirmed that the *Augsburg Confession* had not been refuted, and, using Luther's idea of the *Deus absconditus*, they reminded both the emperor and the Gnesio-Lutherans that God's will cannot be ascertained from actions on battlefields.

> Accordingly, after having been unable to refute our doctrine with God's Word, our opponents may not take very great credit for now having refuted Luther's doctrine with the sword (nor can they assert that we must now all be the more wrong since they have all the power and the upper hand. Accordingly too, devout God-fearing people should not be angry, nor should they either now or in the future go so far as to lose confidence in this teaching. God has always acted in this way. When the prophets, Christ, and the apostles and other Christian teachers after them, as now presently, were suppressed and killed, this is the very time when their teaching first began to burst forth . . . since [God] affects *strength even in weakness, living even in dying, and honor even in shame*, and whereas men are intending to eradicate His word and His name; in spite of them and to their shame He looks to the planting of His Word and Name.[16]

The Magdeburg pastors averred that the emperor's forces might win battles, but that fact did not mean they were right. Lutherans must not give up hope because God's Word will not be overcome by the sword.[17]

Considering these two premises—that the emperor disturbs the peace and the evangelical position remains intact—the Lutheran pastors outlined their third position: why lesser magistrates ought to resist. In doing this they establish a right to resist based on natural law and divine Law, a two-tiered argument rooted in Luther's *Warning*. They also issued a warning to those who would either aid the foe or fail to support them in their cause. They referred to the pope as the antichrist, portrayed Luther as Elijah, and compared those who opposed them to the "prophets of Baal." They made clear that those who oppose the *Augsburg Confession* oppose Christ.[18] A final warning to those who sided with the "Antichrist" or who remained on the sidelines summarizes their position:

> We wish to issue an admonition and warning to all godfearing supe-riors and their subjects . . . [that] they are not able to give help or sup-port to our persecutors without guilt in the sight of God . . . and it is at the peril of both their temporal and their eternal destruction not only if they help to bring about our destruction but also if they com-pletely abandon us.[19]

In concluding their brief introduction, the pastors underlined a funda-mental doctrine that supported their work: They referred, though not by name, to Luther's doctrine of the two kingdoms. Their readers were to resist the current persecution, "each one in accordance with his calling and his ability."[20] The implication, to be repeated again and again in the body of the work, is that persons ought to work in their areas of competence and calling; lesser magistrates must resist,[21] and pastors must admonish and preach.[22]

"CONFESSION"

That the city of Magdeburg's political resistance in 1550 represented a continuation of Luther's thought is best seen in the fact that the doctrine of the two kingdoms and the *theologia crucis* serve as the axiom to *The Magdeburg Confession*. In each section of the document, key connections to Luther's theological presuppositions appear, which strongly influenced the Magdeburg pastors.

The *Confession* begins with a recapitulation of the *Augsburg Confession*,[23] setting forth the context of the resistance to the emperor. The resistance is not because of current political disagreements, though political consid-erations may have conspired with religious fervor. The reason for resis-tance rested in *doctrine*:

> We recognize our responsibility to send forth in print this testimony
> in order that God may be given due honor and that poor oppressed
> Christians may see that such witness is not completely extinguished
> and that there still exists here a small band who, meanwhile, still hold
> to him and if Christ will confer upon them His Spirit, His grace, and
> His strength, who will continue to hold out with Him to the very end,
> praying too that He may of His grace bring back those who have gone
> astray and fallen. Amen.[24]

The pastors' battle was a fight to defend the Gospel, which in their opin-ion was under attack overtly by the forces of the Interim and covertly in the capitulation of the Adiaphorists.[25]

Chapter 1 briefly outlines the doctrine of the Trinity. Because there was no disagreement over the Trinity, the chapter is one of the shortest—barely one page—in the *Confession*. Likewise, the second chapter on sin is only two pages. Chapter 3 on the Law and good works, however, is more lengthy: four-and-a-half pages. In this section, the pastors begin their dis-cussion of the use and abuse of authority. In keeping with Luther's theol-ogy of the cross, they assert that authorities are part of God's order *in cre-ation*,[26] a role that is part of God's general revelation and that belongs to all authorities—even non-Christian rulers are responsible to God for the maintenance of justice. They are to be a terror to "wicked rascals" and allow "honest, upright citizens" the opportunity to enjoy all sorts of "tem-poral goods." Ultimately, the maintenance of order serves God because it creates an environment in which preachers can proclaim the Gospel with-out obstruction.

Once they had set out a correct understanding of authority's use of the Law, the Magdeburg pastors turned their attention to misuses of the Law. In keeping with Luther's doctrine of the two kingdoms, they delineated two major errors concerning the Law. The first, made by Anabaptists, was to see the promulgation and observance of law as antithetical to the Gospel.[27] The second error, made by the "papists," was to conflate the Law and the Gospel by making them into one, thereby denying each its prop-er role. The pastors later return to this subject at length in their discussion of temporal authority.

The next chapter on the Gospel is one of the longest in the *Confession*. It focuses on a major area of disagreement between the Gnesio-Lutherans and the supporters of the emperor. Its 12 pages begin by outlining the works of Christ, his righteousness, and justification by faith alone. The point the pastors attempt to articulate is that humanity has nothing to offer God; we can only receive Christ.[28] The Gospel is a gift to be received, not a treasure to be earned. From this understanding, the pastors make the point that one cannot force another to accept such a gift.

Following their positive discussion of the Gospel and justification, the authors turn their attention to some of the common errors made when considering the Gospel and justification. They list and explain 12 major errors, most of which are variations on confusing the Gospel with the Law. One error they discuss is the Roman Catholic error of *praecepta novae legis* (precepts of a new law) whereby the Roman delegation had "out of the Gospel made a sermon on the law with their devilish invented fiction that Christ came to proclaim additional more perfect laws than Moses did."[29] This was one of the central errors Luther identified in his distinction between the Spirit and the letter of the Law.[30] When viewed as law, the Gospel is a terror to the soul because it is a new and harsher Law. This undermines the Law's true role—showing the futility of works righteousness—and leads only to despair and *Anfechtungen*.

The pastors also outlined the other fundamental mistake concerning the Law and the Gospel: perceiving the law as the way to salvation. The pastors, echoing Luther, outlined the danger in this mistake:

> [The Roman theologians] have completely removed from the Gospel the promise that God will receive us back to grace without all our merits, solely for the sake of Christ. Thereby they have removed any distinction between the law and the Gospel thus completely removing the true Gospel, depriving Christ of His due honor and they have given that honor to their own wretched miserable works, and thus entirely robbed poor, weak, timorous, tried, and tempted consciences of their only true consolation.[31]

In Roman theology, Christ is reduced to an example to be emulated.[32]

The Adiaphorists did not fare much better. In some ways the Magdeburg pastors were even sharper when condemning the positions espoused by the adiaphorist party. They have seen the light, the *Confession* notes, but have chosen darkness. They should know better than to confuse the Gospel with the Law, yet they do:

> They make no distinction where it is most vital to do so, at this juncture, between infused righteousness and the justification of one's own works and the third party righteousness of Christ which is credited to

us through faith. Accordingly they glossed over the main point in this negotiation, the basic distinction which shows the fundamental difference between the pure doctrine of the Gospel and the teaching of the papists or Interimists.[33]

Failing to maintain the distinction between two kinds of righteousness, the Adiaphorists proceed to err in regard to the power of good works and one's "natural strength and power and free will to follow God in obedience." In other words, they have completely abandoned the reformation of Luther.[34]

In the fifth chapter, the authors reexamine the evangelical position on the sacraments. Here they deal with Baptism, the Eucharist, and Absolution, skillfully demonstrating the *Lutheran* character of their theology. The bulk of the chapter is an outline of mistakes concerning the nature of the sacraments. The writers defined their position as contrary to the errors of the Anabaptists and Roman Catholics; both groups misunderstand the essential nature of sacraments and both make gifts from God into works of man.

The Anabaptists err by placing no real efficacy in the sacraments, focusing instead on human rationality and judgment in their rejection of infant baptism. This emphasis on human capabilities and effort undermines the nature of the sacraments as a "means of grace." It places priority on the works of man as a rational being. For Anabaptists, the sacrament is not important because of what God does, but because of what the individual being baptized thinks about the baptism. The pastors also deride the Roman doctrine of *ex opere operato* as antithetical to justification by faith. Here the issue is not what one *thinks*, but what one *does*. The very act of walking through the motions is enough. The focus is again on humanity and not on God.

In the sixth chapter, the theologians outline the nature of the church. With Luther, they saw the world as a battleground between God and the devil. The devil has allies in sin and death, while God has Christ and the church. The pastors' definition of the church is short and simple: "God has willed that a Church be gathered together of the human race to oppose the serpent."[35] The pastors then define the tools the church has at its disposal in its battle against the serpent. They echo Luther's two kingdoms doctrine. The proper function of the church is to proclaim the Word and administer the sacraments. Anything else is inappropriate for a spiritual struggle. The pastors write:

> God forestalls the Devil by the gifts of the office of the Word and of the Sacraments, which office he also makes effective only in those

among this contingent of people who hear the Word and make use of the sacraments.

Using the gifts of their office inappropriately turns the "very ones . . . who should be teaching, governing, and protecting the church [into] enemies of the true church."[36]

The discussion of the gifts of office led the Magdeburg pastors into a lengthy presentation on the power of the keys, an expression drawn from Matt 16:18–19.[37] As early as the Patristic period, the phrase "keys of the kingdom of heaven" was interpreted as giving the church the authority to forgive sins. Over time, however, the power of the keys was restricted—for all practical purposes—to the pope and was expanded to imply authority over not just sin, but all civil and ecclesial administration. The Magdeburg pastors assail both the restriction of the power of the keys exclusively to the pope and the expansion of that power. Then they define the proper interpretation of Matt 16:19:

> The power of the keys consists in the following: it requires the hold-er to teach the Word of God, to serve the Sacraments, to loose or to bind the sins of individuals, or of many people, appoint servants of the church, to examine and judge questions of religion, see to the keep-ing of good order in the church, all things necessary or helpful in the office commanded by Christ. To do all those things as a whole or indi-vidually brings the power of the keys with it, yet in such a way that it should not be done chiefly and according to human wisdom or judg-ment, but rather according to the command and Word of God, for the building up of the Church, not the destroying of it, for the living alone, and not for the dead.[38]

After defining the role of the keys, the pastors note that there is a proper role for authority and oversight within the church. However, this oversight or authority is limited to the ordering of the life *of the church*. It does not extend to other spheres of life. Again, the pastors echoed Luther's distinctions in his doctrine of the two kingdoms. The church has a role in God's creation—to preach and administer the sacraments. Some authori-ty, obviously, must exist, but limiting that authority to one person alone is improper, and expanding that authority into other spheres of ordinance is equally improper.[39]

Following their discussion of the right use and abuse of church author-ity, the pastors move on to the right use and abuse of secular authority. In chapter 7, "Temporal and Domestic Rule and Power," the *Confession* makes assertions about civil and family governance drawn from Luther. God establishes the authorities to limit the power of sin and chaos. One of the principal duties of civil authority is to maintain an environment of civility and calm so the Gospel might be preached. The government does not serve the church *per se*, as the pastors believe that the "papists" assert. The government serves God, who desires that everyone should hear the Gospel. The distinction is fine but nonetheless vital. The government does not serve at the whimsy of church officials. Instead, it cooperates with the church in God's plan for the redemption of creation.[40]

The fundamental question that confronted the Magdeburg pastors in their current situation was what happens when an institution turns from its proper role to an improper one? The pastors wanted to be clear: They did not wish to give carte blanche to general resistance. They stated repeatedly that subjects "must be obedient to their authorities."[41] This obedience, though, is not blind. It has limits that must be acknowledged and respected. In principle, then, the pastors return to the function of governance: It must serve God's regulation of chaos in the created world.[42] When authorities, whether parents in the home or the lord of the estate, abandon this function of limiting evil and protecting the good; when authorities terrorize the good, turn their subjects away from honorable living, and forbid the proclamation of the Gospel,

> Then they dispose of their own honor and they can no longer be considered as authorities or parents either before God nor in the conscience of their subjects. They become an ordinance of the devil instead of God, and ordinance which everyone can and ought to resist with a good conscience, each in accordance with his calling.[43]

Given these limits on authority, the pastors sum up their understanding of the proper relationship of authority: It serves God by limiting evil and encouraging the good.

The pastors conclude the chapter by condemning three improper understandings of civil authority. First, they condemn the Anabaptists—who forbid participation in government—for rejecting the good and proper role of government as part of God's plan for creation. Second, they condemn papal authorities who diminish the proper role of government by seeking to usurp its authority. Third, they condemn those who

> Go to the other extreme in being of the opinion that authority is completely above punishment and no one dare resist, even if it represses the good which it ought to honor, and on the other hand upholds and honors the evil which it should punish.[44]

The pastors end the chapter by promising to "deal further in the following part of this small book" with the third, and to their mind, most serious error.

The *Confession* seeks to assure readers of two points. First, everything the pastors have said is grounded upon the "prophets and the apostles."[45] Second, their positions represent the continuation of Martin Luther's thought. The text refers readers to Luther's legacy for support of their argument[46] and frequently quotes or refers to Luther's writing.

"THE INSTRUCTION OF JUSTIFIED RESISTANCE"

Apart from Scripture, Luther is the only theological or historical source regularly quoted in *The Magdeburg Confession*. Of the Reformer's many treatises and writings, only one is mentioned more than once—*Dr. Martin Luther's Warning to His Dear German People*.

Elector Maurice of Saxony, c. 1550.

Luther wrote the *Warning* in 1530 when he thought the emperor was going to attack the Protestant estates. In 1550, the emperor, through his surrogate the Elector Maurice, already had attacked the city of Magdeburg. Thus, Luther's treatise was a natural source to look to for support. Yet a key question remains: Did Luther simply contribute the rhetorical structure of the *Confession* or did he genuinely provide theological substance for the document? We already have demonstrated the document's heavy dependence on Luther in the "Confession" section. Is this also true in the final section? Did the Magdeburg pastors call on Luther but act like Thomas Müntzer?

The pastors refer to the *Warning* at the beginning of the document (A3r) and at the conclusion (O2v). These references are not contrived, but attest to the pastors' continuation of Luther's legacy. Nowhere is this assertion more obvious than in "The Instruction of Justified Resistance."[47]

The Magdeburg Confession is strikingly similar to Luther's *Warning to His Dear German People*. Each has three sections: a survey of the present situation and the theological issues at stake, an apology for just resistance, and a warning. Each is written to a similar audience; both documents were written to encourage the convicted and to convict the undecided. *The Magdeburg Confession* also places its justification for resistance on the same *notoria iniuria* (great injury) as Luther used in the *Warning*.

Rooted in the Justinian Code, the principle of great injury released lesser magistrates from their fealty to the emperor and freed them to resist. In every case since the *Torgau Declaration*, the injury noted was the unlawful regulation of religion by the emperor. Given this application to their situation, the pastors reaffirmed Luther's three-pronged foundation for justified resistance: (1) the natural law argument that resistance is not rebellion, (2) the positive law allowance for justified resistance, and (3) the conviction that the proclamation of the Gospel is at stake. In each, the distinction made between an order of the devil and an order of God is integral.

For the positive law argument, the pastors did not restate the *Torgau Declaration*'s position. They took for granted the right of lesser magistrates to resist. This reflects the progress of Lutheran theory in the 1530s and 1540s. During that period, Luther, Melanchthon, and others became more comfortable with the idea of resistance by lesser magistrates.[48]

INTRODUCTION

The pastors needed to establish the position that their resistance was defensive in nature. They used Luther's three insights to frame their assertions. First, they had continually sought peace and had never violated any imperial laws. Second, because they had not violated any law, the emperor is the peace-breaker and, therefore, the true rebel against order. Third, they cannot be condemned or attacked without a fair hearing. From the perspective of the pastors, rebellion requires breaking the peace and a violation of imperial law. Defense, on the other hand, is the act of innocents unjustly denied due process; injury or abuse prompts defense.

The pastors begin their argument by restating the central belief that they "adhere to pure doctrine." They frame this assertion against both the Adiaphorists and the papists. The pastors condemn the Adiaphorists for sheepishly capitulating to the emperor and abandoning the true Gospel. Then they ask how the Adiaphorists can in "good conscience" condemn Magdeburg for fearlessly maintaining true evangelical theology. The pastors remind their readers (referring again to Flacius's slogan) that if one is forced into sin (or for that matter sheepisly capitulates to it), then doctrine cannot be an indifferent thing.[49]

The pastors made these assertions to undermine the Adiaphorists' claim that they are merely troublemakers and stirrers of dissent. On the contrary, the pastors want simply to preach the true doctrine; they do not need to justify themselves in the eyes of the Adiaphorists because "we Christians for the sake of doctrines and ceremonies cannot be rightfully condemned and attacked."[50] They should not, and cannot with any sense of justice, be physically attacked for their preaching. The same position holds true in relation to the Roman Catholic theologians. The pastors stand convicted as heretics and are excommunicated in the eyes of the Catholics. Even if they were heretics and wrong, they are still suffering injustice because they have never been given a hearing. The lack of a hearing nullifies their conviction. Therefore, in the war against the Magdeburg pastors, the emperor does not, in essence, have solid legal foundations.[51] The Catholics know this, which is why they fight so vehemently. They must silence the protest of the pastors or face their own complicity in the emperor's sin.[52]

Yet the pastors would not keep silent. They knew their legal rights. Even if others have given up (a veiled allusion to Melanchthon) and forsaken the right to a just hearing, this does not mean that their "poor small despised little group lose [their] rights by default."[53] The pastors state that they wished no harm toward anyone, they desired no land, nor did they covet anyone's goods; therefore, the attack on the city was unwarranted.

However, before they advocate resistance, good Christian conscience impels them first to appeal to the emperor himself.

The appeal to the emperor has an almost revolving pattern of argument. The pastors explore a topic, move on, return to it from a different side, move on, and so forth. Although the appeal may seem redundant, the authors are attempting to build an airtight case for the defensive nature of their resistance.

The pastors' appeal to the emperor, in 12 full pages, constitutes the largest portion of the "Instruction." The text changes frequently from the first person plural to the second person singular. This section is a conversation in which the authors' try to convince the emperor of two central points. First, they are not a political threat. Second, because they are not a threat, it is unjust to attack them. The authors examine the rights, responsibilities, and limits of the secular realm. Regarding the rights of the emperor, they recognize that the emperor is the legitimate ruler of this temporal estate. The emperor has been entrusted with the German Empire, but Christ's church makes no claim on either the emperor's land or his possessions. As Christ's servants, all the pastors seek is the freedom to preach.[54]

The second right the pastors examined was the emperor's legitimate demand for obedience and loyalty. His people must be subject for three reasons: (1) God has placed the emperor above them, and to honor the emperor is to give honor to God. (2) They must fear secular judgment and punishment. The emperor has at his disposal the "sword" that can—in fact, must—be used to maintain law and order. (3) They must fear God, referring back to the first rationale—God has ordered creation, so those who flaunt that command risk a withholding of grace or even eternal punishment. The pastors conclude this paragraph by assuring the emperor that they continue to preach that a Christian's duty is obedience and loyalty to the emperor. In fact, they stated that if their petition for grace is granted, the emperor will not find, anywhere in his lands, more loyal and thankful subjects.

The pastors next discuss the emperor's responsibilities to his subjects. His central responsibility, in light of Romans 13, is to be a terror to the bad and a commendation to the good. The pastors use this discussion of the emperor's responsibilities to feature his shortcomings as a ruler. The pastors note with sadness that in the current situation the emperor is a terror to the good, not the bad. The pastors highlight the emperor's injustice in not allowing them the freedom to preach. This freedom is not denied to even "heathens"—for the emperor has within his realm "Jews and other heathens whom [he] does not force from their religion."[55] By failing to be consistent, the emperor is not only unjust, he is unreasonable. The reasonable exercise of the secular realm is a key element in Luther's two kingdom's doctrine.

The pastors draw on an allusion meant to disturb the conscience of the emperor. Even if the emperor disagrees with them, by unjustly persecuting them (when he doesn't even persecute heathens) he is placing himself in the company of the high priests who condemned Christ, Pilate who allowed Christ's execution, and the emperors of old who persecuted and martyred the saints. They also allude to Luther's *Invocavit Sermons* when they state that the true church "has never forced anybody to the faith by the sword."[56] Preaching the Gospel spreads the faith; using the sword courts terrible judgment. If the emperor does not want to be linked with Pilate, he must cease his war of unjust aggression.[57]

The pastors then return to their assertion that they are loyal and obedient servants of the emperor. This time, however, they included an important and substantial caveat: *They owe primary allegiance to God.* They maintain that:

> This obedience both to God and to the emperor does not mean being against secular authority, not being against one or the other, but means giving one another a hand and can be done with a clear conscience on both sides without uprising or revolt in a good and Christian manner, if they remain in their **proscribed bounds [*termino præscripto*]**, that is, that to each is given what he is entitled to receive.[58]

A significant aspect of Luther's two kingdoms doctrine is the importance of not mixing the secular and spiritual realms. Each has important roles and responsibilities—the magistrate to rule, the church to proclaim the Gospel. For either to interfere with the other is a prescription for disaster and tyranny. In the minds of the pastors, the emperor already has courted this disaster by usurping what is God's alone—the proclamation of the Gospel. By using the sword to force capitulation, the emperor has "transgressed far beyond the bounds of his Imperial Majesty's Empire, office, and command and has encroached upon the Kingdom and Jurisdiction of Christ."[59]

The pastors emphasize that they are loyal and honorable subjects. On this they are willing to stake their reputations, not just for themselves but also for the city of Magdeburg, her city council, and her burgesses. But they will not give homage to the emperor when it belongs to God alone.[60] This usurpation finally forces the pastors' hand. The emperor may be a poor emperor and deny them a right to preach; he may even persecute them for their proclamation; however, by usurping God's prerogative and forcing them into sinful acts, he leaves them no alternative.[61]

In keeping with what is a genuinely positive assessment of imperial authority and their pledge to preach the truth to the powerful, the pastors beg the emperor to cease his unjust ban on the city of Magdeburg and rescind the Augsburg Interim.[62] If the emperor does not rescind his orders and repent of his sin, he risks eternal damnation[63] and will have only himself to blame when lesser magistrates resist him.[64]

At this point, the text takes a dramatic turn. The tenor of the argument remains impassioned, yet there is a palpable reluctance. For the first time the pastors touch on resistance in concrete terms; they tie their objections to particular misdeeds by the emperor and put forth a demand: the revocation of the Interim. The enormity of their claims and discussion is evident. They do not take this situation lightly. They do not relish this role, but neither will they shirk their duty. The pastors do not willingly speak of resistance, and they state frankly that they are afraid others will misunderstand their positions. They are afraid that because the emperor is unjust and persecutes illegally, others will feel inappropriately justified in resistance because of "impatience or feelings of vengeance."[65] Nevertheless, they must speak. In speaking, they cast themselves in the role of the Maccabees against the emperor's Antiochus.[66] Like the Seleucid king, Charles V wanted to destroy true worship of the Lord. He lay siege to an innocent city and sought to destroy God's children.[67] But like the Maccabees, the pastors of Magdeburg will not sit by silently. As in the time of the Maccabeans, God-fearing men and women in Magdeburg felt that God forbids resistance. But like Judas Maccabeus, the pastors will correct this misconception because they will not allow their flock to be slaughtered.

> Our station, office and in this case similarly the imminent great distress and danger to our and to all churches require that we free the hearts of pious Christians from the cruel vain illusory terrors and teach and console them of the error of the reproach that is made if one dare not defend oneself or stand against authority even against unjust great violence. We must, ought, and will exhort and urge all our Christians in the true doctrine . . . to preserve it for us and those who follow us, they must also fight and struggle and battle with body and life trusting that God is on our side as with the Maccabees.[68]

Up to this point, the risk of being misunderstood kept the pastors silent. Now, because of the siege laid against their city, the risk of remaining silent is too great.[69] This exigency calls on them to outline three arguments for just resistance, each rooted in Luther's theology.

THE ARGUMENTS FOR RESISTANCE

Order and Chaos

The first argument for just resistance was based on Luther's two kingdoms distinction between order and chaos. In an ongoing battle between God and the devil, God has created two realms for the protection of creation and the limitation of chaos. The spiritual and secular realms cooperate with each other in this divine imperative. Each has an appropriate role. The church must proclaim the Word of God and administer the sacraments. The state must limit evil and punish the wicked. Thus, government's authority, like the church's, is given by God.

The pastors support this statement by quoting Romans 13 and Paul's definition of the role of secular government: "the ruler is an ordinance of God to honor the righteous and punish the wicked."[70] How then should Christians deal with an emperor who is unjustly persecuting them?

At times, the pastors assert, government will turn to tyranny, as it has under Charles V. By forsaking his proper role, a tyrant ceases to be an ordinance of God for creating order and limiting chaos and becomes, instead, an ordinance of the devil. When this happens, lesser magistrates are called on by justice and God's command to limit evil and promote good.

When resistance is necessary, so, too, is the requirement that one not confuse one's God-given authority with another's. The tyranny of a superior magistrate does not excuse lower magistrates (in this case the superior magistrate is the emperor's accessory—Maurice, the Elector of Saxony—and the lower magistrates are the city councillors) from their responsibility to promote good and punish evil. They must continue to punish evil, *even if it is in the superior magistrate.*[71]

How does the lesser magistracy rebuke or resist the sin in a superior? To answer that question, the pastors outlined a four-level distinction of tyranny and just response or resistance.

The first degree of injustice concerns "small mean things" (e.g., vices, sexual immorality, etc.). At this level the lesser magistrate should endure injury with patience and "exhort the superior to desist from such undertakings."[72]

The second degree of injustice deals with "great injury" in which the higher authority may wage an unjust war and deny the lesser magistrate home, health, family, or life. The pastors note that one should let God vindicate the abused or only defend those helpless to defend themselves. Here again, the pastors allude to Luther's teaching that it is best if a Christian resists in defense of others but not for one's own benefit.[73]

The third degree of injustice pertains to a magistrate commanded *as a magistrate* to violate God's laws. Here the higher authority—a divine Law—requires that the magistrate resist.[74] In this case, the lower magistrate may resist in two ways. First, he may take the road of what is now considered civil disobedience and simply refuse to obey the command. Or the lower magistrate may raise the sword against the superior. However, the pastors advise that before taking the second step, the lesser magistrate first consult their fourth degree of tyranny. If superiors are "found guilty there then they are indeed tyrants."[75]

At the fourth degree, the tyrant tramples on not just secular rights, does not merely compel one to sin, but also grievously sins against God. Such a tyrant must be resisted:

> When tyrants become so foolish and mad that they begin to attack with weapons and war not only the persons of the inferior magistrates and of their subjects in a righteous matter, but also to attack in their persons at the same time our Lord God Himself, who is Creator of these same laws . . . he is not only a werewolf (to which Luther in his disputation likens to a tyrant), but the devil himself who, if he were there in his own person, can not sin more grievously nor shamefully, only that he does so more wittingly, and that is the true essence and being and indeed the form and effect of government in the kingdom of the devil.[76]

The pastors refer to Luther by using his term *werewolf* to identify a truly renegade tyrant. However, the import of this paragraph is the dichotomy set up between the devil and God. The pastors were able to interpret and apply Paul's command to be subject to authority by demonstrating that the tyrant who opposes God is an ordinance of the devil. Such a tyrant, therefore, fails to be a part of God's ordering of creation and, instead, is in league with chaos. By failing this test, the tyrant ceases to be a legitimate ruler and, therefore, can be resisted.

In fact, the pastors argue that such resistance honors God. A suitable illustration might be a husband and father defending the honor of his wife and daughters. In such a case, a man rightly defends his family and moreover does an honorable thing.[77] Likewise, when a tyrant overthrows God's honor and denies people the Gospel,[78] the people who resist are "not only doing what is right but are doing a special work as a divine task for the honor of God."[79]

Termino Præscripto 1: Mandate

These arguments for just resistance are based on Luther's two kingdoms requirement that each realm has a proper mandate (the second argument) and office (the third argument) in the ordering of creation.[80] The pastors admonish readers that one realm should not encroach on the other; each realm should complement the other.

For the pastors, this complementary relationship is defined by Jesus in Matt 22:21.[81] In the case of Magdeburg, the emperor has received what he is rightly owed. The pastors are not a political threat, but loyal subjects. Yet "Christ does not wish the emperor to be given what is God's."[82] By demanding practices that are, in the opinion of the pastors, an "inducement to sin," the emperor requires what does not belong to his mandate as emperor. The *Confession* likens his demands to the Empress Justine, who demanded the admittance of Arians to church but who was rightly resisted by Ambrose.

The pastors note that the usurpation of what is owed to God may also render the emperor's legitimate demands (e.g., obedience) null and void. They again compare the situation to a family.[83] If a father is unrighteous and returns home with a band of scoundrels intent on dishonoring his wife and daughters, the wife and mother is justified in denying the husband that which normally is his right—admittance to his own home. Instead, she ought to resist him and "even cast stones at him to drive him away."[84] So, too, the people of Magdeburg must deny the emperor what is rightfully his (obedience) when that obedience is contrary to the obedience owed to God.

Termino Præscripto 2: Office

In the final section, the pastors continue their argument of proscribed bounds. The emperor has legitimate demands and a legitimate office or vocation. But he has overstepped his bounds by demanding that which belongs to God. He also has transgressed these bounds by using the sword improperly. In each case, whether it is demands or office, there are legitimate limits to what one may do. When the limits of one's office are obeyed and adhered to, order is preserved and fostered. However, like demanding that which is not one's own, overstepping the limits of one's vocation cultivates chaos and injustice. In such cases, God's very nature demands action. According to the pastors, God's nature is just, loving, omnipotent, omniscient, and immutable. Resistance by lesser magistrates is required because it is an absurdity to think that God would allow human beings to corrupt his order and go unpunished. For God to allow a tyrant to attack the proclamation of the Gospel and go unpunished implies that God was protecting evil and "preventing good." In the opinion of the pastors, this scenario makes God seem not only ambivalent, but capricious. God's purposes would be self-contradictory, an impossible proposition.

God will act. He may act by striking the tyrant down through some illness or the like. He may use another tyrant to overthrow the first. On occasion, "God punishes in such a way that those who execute the punishment are not doing wrong but are carrying out God's will and command."[85] This participation in God's punishment is possible because God has given to all magistrates—not just the highest authority—the vocation and responsibility of "exercising revenge and upholding protection."

The section concludes with a number of short paragraphs in which the pastors outline a number of historic examples of lesser magistrates who resisted the injustice of a superior. They draw from the Old Testament and deuterocanonical books the stories of the Maccabeans and the people's rescue of Saul's condemned son, Jonathan (1 Sam 14:45). They also look to imperial and ecclesiastical history. The careful style of the *Confession* is evident here; each example is carefully documented and explained. In a somewhat ironic twist, the pastors begin by highlighting the excommunication of Emperor Theodosius by Ambrose[86] as an example of a lesser magistrate rebuking or resisting a superior. The irony, of course, is that in succeeding generations and centuries imperial power was viewed as derived from ecclesial authority.

The pastors also appeal to the example of Emperor Trajan (A.D. 98–117). Although a "heathen" emperor, Trajan supported their cause because he sanctioned the right of a lesser magistrate to resist by commanding his subordinate, "Insofar as I command what is right wield this sword against my foes, but if I do the contrary then wield it against myself."[87]

In this section, then, the pastors lay out a foundation for the right, indeed the responsibility, of lesser magistrates to resist the unjust actions of their superior. They appeal to positive law, natural law, and their view that the Gospel itself is at stake. Next, they turn their attention to strengthening the resolve of those defending the Gospel, warning those who side against them, and urging others still on the fence to support their cause.

"ADMONITION AND WARNING"

Shorter than the previous two sections, the "Warning" section of the *Confession* is the rhetorical culmination of the pastors' thought. Everything else has been prolegomena. In their recapitulation of the *Augsburg Confession*, the authors establish and reinforce their contention that they have not wavered from "pure Christian doctrine." In the "Instruction," the pastors establish the justice of their defense of pure doctrine. The "Warning" sets out why one risks one's soul by attacking them and makes the argument in support of joining their defense.

Beginning with the position that to oppose the Reformation is to oppose the Gospel and Christ, the Magdeburg pastors state categorically that one cannot call oneself a Christian and at the same time aid the Interim. Because the church is Christ's body, to attack "poor Christians" by aiding the Interim is to persecute Christ.[88] To persecute Christ allies one with the devil and risks a judgment as harsh as the judgment that will be accorded to Satan and the demonic forces. At this point the pastors refer to the crucifixion of Christ. Although the Roman and Jewish authorities may not have known that crucifying Jesus meant crucifying the Son of God, the Interimists and Adiaphorists have no such excuse.

Attacking the reforms of the church begun by Luther aids the devil because it overthrows all the good that these reforms have accomplished. The Word of God had been preached to many and already had freed many from captivity to papal excesses. The pastors beg those who would march against them to reconsider: Do they really want to undermine the work of God? Do they really want to banish "true doctrine" from the empire?

For Christians to attack fellow Christians is the worst possible sin. Instead, they ought to emulate St. Maurice (Moritz), leader of the Thebian Legion, and refuse the immoral demands of the emperor.[89] According to the legend of St. Maurice, a Christian legion was ordered by the Emperor Diocletian to sacrifice to the gods of Rome. Upon their refusal, they were first decimated, then massacred. From the perspective of the pastors, if one is unable to defend the Gospel, then it is better to be a martyr than "end up in the position of having helped to make others into martyrs."[90]

Yet the armies facing Magdeburg are not caught like the Thebian Legion, unarmed and overwhelmed by force. They must make a decision: Choose this day whom you shall serve, God or the Interim! Although neutrality may appear to be just and even righteous, it is neither because it enables sin to increase:

> Saul's guardians were not guiltless in the eyes of God in that they did
> not themselves strangle the guiltless priests of Nob, and in that they
> did not acquiesce in such murder. But they shared in the guilt for their
> deaths if only because they did not come to their assistance and help
> to save them.[91]

Neutrality is not really neutrality at all because it gives false comfort to the
soul while at the same time aiding and abetting the opposition. For the
pastors of Magdeburg, neutrality, when engaged in a battle with the devil,
was not an option. If the opposition persecutes Christ, and neutrality is the
moral equivalent of persecution, what should a Christian magistrate do?
The pastors framed their answer by quoting Prov 24:11–12:

> If you hold back from rescuing those taken away to death, those who
> go staggering to the slaughter; if you say, "Look, we did not know
> this"—does not he who weighs the heart perceive it? Does not he who
> keeps watch over your soul know it? And will he not repay all accord-
> ing to their deeds?

Friends must come to the rescue of Magdeburg because it is the only
option open to those who consider themselves Christian. Those who do
not aid the pastors in their time of trial are "not true members of the body
of Christ,"[92] and they will face a severe and wrathful judgment for their
inaction. For proof of this terrible judgment, one need only look at Judges
5: God came to the rescue of one tribe of ancient Israel and delivered its
members through a miraculous display of power. When the other tribes of
Israel came to celebrate, they were rebuked for their failure to help. God,
the righteous judge, soon proved how he views such iniquity. He ordered
the other towns, who sat idly by, to be cursed by his angel, "because they
did not come to the help of the LORD, to the help of the LORD against the
mighty" (Judg 5:23). The angel of the Lord accused them not of abandoning their brothers, but of abandoning God himself, despite claims to
be his people.[93]

For other cities and Christian rulers to remain inactive in the current
crisis is a sin not just against Magdeburg, but against God. To avoid this
sin, the pastors outlined four avenues of service that lesser magistrates
should render Magdeburg in her time of distress. First, they ought to pray
for her. Prayer is a strong and effective weapon in any Christian's arsenal
against the devil. Second, they must intercede with the erring superior on
behalf of the city and her citizens. The pastors remind the reader that
Christ orders Christians to lay down their lives for their brethren. In their
opinion, asking lesser magistrates to speak on their behalf is a small

request.[94] Third, if that petition fails (and the pastors fully expect that it will fail), the lesser magistrates ought to emulate Jonathan (1 Samuel 20), who warned David of Saul's intent to kill him. Thus, the lesser magistrates must warn the city in case of attack. Fourth, the magistrates must come and actively defend Magdeburg because it is the only just course to follow. Timidity is not an excuse. Furthermore, magistrates cannot assert that the fight for Magdeburg is not their responsibility. An attack on Christ is an attack on all Christians, regardless of where it happens. The city is confident that God shall prevail, but even if one dies in defense of the city, one dies a martyr's and saint's death. Death will find each and every person; it is better to die for a cause than to die a coward and enemy of God.[95]

The pastors conclude the *Confession* with a final admonition to obey God's command according to one's calling. They had lived up to their calling by preaching only true doctrine and admonishing the errant. Now the lesser magistrates must follow their lead and punish the wicked. The document closes with a final testament to the pastor's faith: "God will not allow the gates of hell to prevail against his Church."[96] Although they suffer and are "killed all the day long" for the sake of Christ and his church,[97] "heaven and earth shall pass away, but [God's] word will not pass away."[98]

CONCLUSION

The Magdeburg Confession was published in April 1550. On July 27 of the same year, the city's imperial ban was published. In September, the Elector Maurice of Saxony laid siege to the city. However, the city was in the fight for the long haul. Practicing a scorched-earth military tactic, the city's forces set the Neustadt and the Sudenburg on fire. Both sections of the city sat outside the city's great wall. The people of the Neustadt and the Sudenburg were brought into the Altstadt.

The siege of Magdeburg lasted for more than a year. In November 1551, a stalemate of sorts was recognized. Because popular opinion throughout Saxony was quickly moving against him and in favor of the city, Maurice recognized that he could not take Magdeburg. In a striking political change of course, Maurice flipped allegiance. Originally he had been a member of the Schmalkaldic League, but he switched sides to gain the emperor's goodwill and the electoral dignity of Saxony. Now, to solidify his rule, he switched sides again.

The city was then occupied. Maurice claimed victory, with a few minor concessions, such as the preservation of the *Augsburg Confession*. However, to this day, the city of Magdeburg holds that the city was never defeated (*Ergeben*).[99] Instead, the city reached a "coming-to-terms" (*Vertragen*) with Maurice.[100]

The stalemate of Magdeburg brought to an end the medieval ideal of a *corpus christianum*. Duke Maurice's change of allegiance, as well as internal discord among the Habsburgs, spelled the end of Charles V's crusade against the Protestant estates. Charles had a small window of opportunity; he lost that opportunity at the walls of Magdeburg.

In 1555, a final settlement between Charles and the Protestant princes was approved at Augsburg. The Peace of Augsburg recognized the central claim of the Magdeburg pastors and the *Torgau Declaration*—religious diversity does not equal imperial disloyalty. The Augsburg Interim reinforced princely authority and, for the first time, gave legal imperial sanction to Lutheran reforms. The Peace of Augsburg did not, however, grant anything close to religious tolerance. Instead, what it did allow was local control of religion by local princes—a settlement that would reach final formulation around 1600 in the phrase *cuius regio, eius religio* (who reigns, his religion). The grand hope of a unified, homogeneous Christian empire died at Magdeburg, as did Luther's hope of reforming the church *catholic*. That dream may well have died moments after Luther nailed his theses to the door, but in Magdeburg and later in Augsburg, nothing remained but the postmortem.

In Luther's larger dream of freedom to proclaim the free grace of God in Jesus Christ, Magdeburg may be counted as a grand success. *The Magdeburg Confession* played a significant role in amassing support for the cause of the city. As Oliver K. Olson

MAGDEBVRGVM, A VENERE QVÆ HIC QVONDAM COLEBATVR PARTHE: NOPOLIS DICTA, *Metropolitica Saxoniæ vrbs, opibus et authoritate memora: bilis, peraugusto murorum ambitu, & Albis fluuij vicinitate illustris.*

notes, to no small degree the defense of Magdeburg preserved Lutheran reforms in Germany. Had Magdeburg not resisted, the Augsburg Interim would have quickly become the religious norm. While giving lip service to the Reformation, the Interim abandoned many of the key elements of Luther's theology. By resisting the Interim, the Gnesio-Lutherans preserved "true" Lutheranism for posterity and provided the first example of a Lutheran theory of political resistance.

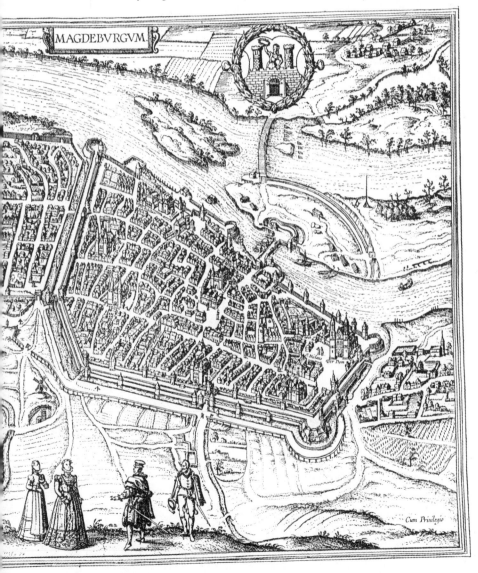

5

CONCLUSION

I am the LORD your God, who brought you out of the land of Egypt, out of the house of slavery; you shall have no other gods before me.—*Exodus 20:1–2*

Today there are once more saints and villains. Instead of the uniform grayness of the rainy day, we have the black storm cloud and brilliant lightning flash. Outlines stand out with exaggerated sharpness. Shakespeare's characters walk among us. The villain and the saint emerge from the primeval depths and by their appearance they tear open the infernal or divine abyss from which they come and enable us to see for a moment into the mysteries of which we had never dreamed.—Dietrich Bonhoeffer, *Ethics*

A LUTHERAN THEORY OF RESISTANCE

The success of Magdeburg in resisting the Interim, in defending the Gospel, and in assuring the continuation of reform make it a potent example of theologically informed political resistance. The foremost question behind this study is *Who informed the theology of the Magdeburgers?* Two dramatically different positions regarding the interplay of state and church were evident at the time. Thomas Müntzer followed a path of convergence; Martin Luther chose clearly demarcated lines of distinction.

Luther attempted to define a proper distinction between the administration of civil affairs and the administration of religion. For him, government did not have to be Christian to be good. Müntzer, on the other hand, argued that government had a responsibility to be Christian and to enforce Christianity. Government was part of God's creative order and had to ensure correspondence in the people to God's Law. Müntzer, then, represents an alternative perspective to Luther. Where Luther sought to maintain a legitimate tension and cooperation between the secular and sacred realms, allowing each freedom from undue influence, Müntzer collapsed the two into his own will. Müntzer's theological legacy is one of theocracy and a cult of personality. If quotes from the *The Magdeburg Confession* are taken out of context, the pastors of Magdeburg can sound similar to Müntzer, but they claimed the legacy of Luther. So whom did they truly follow: Luther or Müntzer?

For people in the late medieval or early Modern Era, religion was not simply a compartmentalized event practiced on Sundays. It was more than just personal piety. It was the lens through which much—if not all—of life was viewed and interpreted. What one believed mattered because it affected how one acted in the world.[1]

The pastors of Magdeburg understood that fact. Their pamphlet was not just a political tract handed out at rallies. It was also a confession of faith that recognized the current political situation as a *status confessionis*. Thus, it responded to a situation that was both political and theological. Magdeburg was not attacked because she refused to pay taxes or because she revolted against the emperor in an attempt to gain land and fortune. Magdeburg was attacked to crush theological "innovation." The pastors' response was to underscore the lines of distinction between the secular and the sacred. The question that must now be answered is whether their confession of faith represents a legacy of Luther.

To answer that question, let's reconsider Luther's main points and examine whether *The Magdeburg Confession* meets Luther's standard. In examining its position, we will also contrast it to the position held by Thomas Müntzer. Müntzer represents a competing theory of theological praxis. We have judged that praxis to be deficient. Did the Magdeburg pastors do so as well?

In all political theories, perceptions about human nature and personal identity form theories of governance and freedom. For example, James Madison argued for a strong central government in *Federalist #10* because, in his opinion, human nature is inherently depraved and the weak need protection. "Brutus," responding in *Anti-Federalist #11*, argued for a weak central government with more local autonomy because human beings are essentially good and thus can be trusted to wield more control over themselves. Luther's and Müntzer's understandings of human nature and Christian identity make a great difference in their positions on resistance to and interaction with governmental authority. For Luther, Christian identity is more veiled than for Müntzer. Müntzer saw the hand of God at work in the world. He argued for, then fought for, the establishment of God's reign. Luther took a different perspective. No less than Müntzer,

Luther knew that God was at work in the world, yet Luther was unwilling to point to particular events or experiences and declare God's will.

For Luther, the cross confounds attempts to discern God's actions as though reading tea leaves. Müntzer had no such hesitance. For him, personal revelation from the Holy Spirit made everything clear. If the elect are truly the elect, they will demonstrate that election by agreeing with his interpretation of God's will. Resistance to an errant magistrate is not resistance at all; it sets things right.

If various parts of the *Confession* are identified and explored in isolation, the Magdeburg pastors sound very similar to Müntzer. They claim that the emperor had revealed himself to be in league with the devil. Resistance to his Interim was not only legal, it was a good thing that would merit God's favor—not in regard to salvation, but in regard to a greater glory in heaven. Have they not, then, abandoned Luther at the most critical juncture in his thought? Have the pastors, like Müntzer, found the magistrate to be forsaking his mandate to establish the Gospel and called for his removal? No, they have not. Although in individual lines or quotations the pastors may sound like Müntzer, they think theologically and argue self-consciously like Luther. With Luther, the pastors recognize that the issue of resistance is serious and a matter of Christian conscience and Christian praxis. To demonstrate this, consider the central motifs present in Luther's theology of the cross.

The first motif is the power of the Word. For Luther, the Word of God is active, the *Deus dixit* elicits a response in the one to whom it is spoken. Luther's reliance on the activity and power of the Word was a primary reason for his opposition to Müntzer's (and Karlstadt's) attempts to impose reform by force. Luther felt that to compel reform undermined preaching and transformed the Gospel into Law. Ministry in the kingdom of Christ, then, is always focused on proclamation, not coercion.

This motif undergirded Luther's natural law foundation for political resistance. From the belief that offensive action to establish the Gospel is never allowed or warranted, Luther argued that resistance must be defensive in nature. In the *Confession*, this motif and its corollary praxis may be seen in the fact that large portions of the work are devoted to the demonstration of the city's loyalty to the emperor and of the defensive nature of their resistance. They return again and again to the point that they do not wish anything that rightfully belongs to the emperor. They merely wish to defend their right to preach.

The second motif is Luther's understanding of the *Deus absconditus*.
For Luther, revelation is hidden and indirect. This, Luther argues,
requires one to be patient when considering resistance. The Christian may
justly resist only when an attack is made on the proclamation of the Gospel
itself because it is only at that level that the superior betrays his allegiance
to the devil. He may usurp land, but the Christian must suffer the injustice. He may overturn law and tradition, but the Christian must suffer. He
may falsely imprison and punish, and the Christian must bear it. In each of
these examples the representative of the state may look unjust and tyrannical from a human perspective (*coram hominibus*) and yet remain just *coram
deo* because he is acting on God's behalf as a punishing judge. However,
when the superior turns and attacks God's own proclamation, when he
subverts the Gospel, then he has betrayed his true colors. He is not a punishing judge, but a *werewolf* roaming the land. Then, and only then, the veil
that shrouds the *Deus absconditus* is lifted slightly and the tyrant can be
resisted.

For Müntzer, revelation is direct; therefore, he has no need to hesitate.
Müntzer himself would have vehemently argued that he was defending the
Gospel. However, because he mixed theology and politics so thoroughly,
it is impossible to discern where Müntzer's adversaries were attacking him
for his theology and where they were attacking him for his political machi-
nations. He was thrown out of Mühlhausen not for his preaching, but
because he attempted a coup d'etat. However unjustifiable the actions of
the princes in the Battle of Frankenhausen, they were not attacking the
proclamation of the Gospel.

For the Magdeburg pastors, as for Luther, the *Deus absconditus* doctrine played a significant role in the construction of their political theology. The most striking example of this is their discussion of injustice and
response. Like Luther, they set out four levels of injustice and their corre-
sponding responses. Unlike Müntzer, at the first three levels of injustice
the response by lesser magistrates remains sinful. Even at level three—
serious injury, where the superior may seek to deprive the lesser of land
and life—the conscience of the lesser magistrate remains conflicted. The
pastors urge restraint at this level. In fact, the superior may be an agent of
God's harsh judgment against the lesser. At this level, natural law and positive law may allow resistance, but God's Law does not. That is why the
pastors encourage the lesser magistrate to wait and consider the fourth
degree of tyranny—defense of the Gospel.

The third motif present in Luther's understanding of Christian identity and in *The Magdeburg Confession* is the distinction between order and
chaos. Integral to this distinction is Luther's understanding of proscribed
bounds (*termino præscripto*). This motif provides the foundation for
Luther's contention that lesser magistrates must lead resistance only
because they also participate in God's ordering of creation. God gives lesser magistrates the same authority as their superiors to limit chaos and to
provide an environment in which to preach the Gospel without hindrance.

Müntzer, however, had no concept of a lesser magistracy. He used any
expedient means available to attain his political and religious goals. First,
he attempted to persuade the princes to follow him. When they declined,
he turned to the peasants. Müntzer did not have a working definition of
political authority beyond that of a cult of personality. Political and religious authority rested in him. He was God's prophet and avenging judge.
Whereas Luther sought to separate the two kingdoms, Müntzer collapsed
them into himself.

On this point, the *Confession* echoes Luther and not Müntzer. The
views of the pastors are entirely consistent with Luther's understanding of
lesser magistrates participating in God's ordering of creation. In fact, a
large portion of the "Instruction" is dedicated to explicating Luther's position in light of current circumstances.

The final and most important motif present in Luther's understanding
of Christian identity is the distinction between Law and Gospel. This
point was equally important to the pastors of Magdeburg because a proper distinction protects both realms. Such a distinction prevents the Law
from becoming sentimentalized or demonized into a quasi-Gospel; it also
prevents the Gospel from becoming regimented into a new Law.

In the arena of church life, this distinction is critical because it safe-
guards the doctrine of salvation by grace. If a new quasi-Law becomes an
avenue for salvation, then grace is supplanted by works. Then what
becomes important in the life of an individual is not dependence on God's
grace, but fidelity to the Law. This becomes even more serious when this
Law attaches itself to a particular political agenda. Whether blatant or
merely implied, there is a propensity to identify one position as the only
"Christian" response. To disagree is to be less than or even non-Christian.
Müntzer followed this path. He found it easy to ordain political events or
figures. They were either for him or against God. Magdeburg followed
Luther's lead and refused to ordain events as God's will.

Luther's point is simple but important. The cross must remain the only avenue to salvation. In Müntzer's system of politics *and* theology, the distinction between government official and Christian, between sin and crime, blur and disintegrate. Contrary to Müntzer, government must pursue potential suspects because they have violated a law, not because they have violated the Ten Commandments. For the government official, as an agent of the state or commonwealth, reason and law must guide decisions and actions, not the Gospel. If the Gospel were the "norm" of political and social behavior, human beings might never experience order and stability, given all the human frailties and failures that surround us daily. This distinction is present in Magdeburg, but it is not desirable or possible for Müntzer. In Müntzer's view, one's Christian duty as a magistrate is to ensure fidelity to God's Law. Instead, the Magdeburg pastors call on magistrates to resist the implementation of laws aimed at inhibiting or destroying the church and its proclamation. If a modern nation passed a law forbidding the celebration of the Lord's Supper, evangelical pastors should call on magistrates to resist enforcement of that law. The issue at stake is not how secular law conforms to the Gospel, but how the Gospel and the church's ministry of Word and Sacrament must be preserved.

What differentiates the Magdeburg pastors' understanding of Christian identity from Müntzer's and aligns the *Confession* with Luther is the willingness to defend *only* the Gospel. Müntzer sought to establish the Gospel through the sword. *The Magdeburg Confession* echoes Luther because only the preaching of the Word can establish the Gospel. The sword turns the Gospel into the Law and, thereby, nullifies it completely. The pastors could not simply identify any action of an unjust ruler and say with certainty, "This is God's will." Only when a ruler betrays his allegiance to the devil by opposing the Gospel is such a distinction possible.

The *Confession*, then, reflects *Luther's* theology. At each point, the pastors demonstrated their fidelity to Luther's position without attempting to blaze a new trail in resistance theory. Because they followed a trail already marked out by Luther, Luther's presence in the *Confession* is not artificial. Nor is his influence and legacy drawn on only for rhetorical support. The pastors were correct in stating that if readers wanted to know more about what they were reading, they should examine Luther's *Warning*.

IMPACT OF THE *CONFESSION*

All European Protestants closely followed the events of the Interim. They recognized that if Charles V succeeded in stamping out the Reformation in the Holy Roman Empire, other rulers (for example, Henry II in France) might be emboldened to follow his example. Therefore Calvin, Bullinger, Beza, and others in Geneva closely followed the situation in Magdeburg. But how closely did they follow Magdeburg's lead? And what of the Marian exiles from England later in the 1550s or the Huguenots in the 1560s and 1570s? Did *The Magdeburg Confession* have a lasting influence on later theologians and church leaders?

In fact, Magdeburg's influence can clearly be seen in at least two individuals: Theodore Beza and John Knox. Beza refers to the *Confession* twice in treatises on government and resistance. Both references come at important junctures in history and shed some light on the influence of Magdeburg. The first reference appears in Beza's tract *On the Punishment of Heretics*, which was written in 1554 after the arrest of Michael Servetus in Geneva. Written largely as a proposal for noble government, Beza discusses the authority and responsibility of lesser magistrates:

> An inferior magistrate, with the greatest caution and moderation, but nonetheless fittingly and wisely, ought to defend true religion in his own realm, insofar as he can do so. The city of Magdeburg, situated on the Elbe, offered the outstanding example of this in our time.[2]

The arrest of Servetus, however, was not the only significant event in Geneva during 1554. In 1553, Mary Tudor succeeded her half brother Edward VI to the English throne and quickly reinstated Catholicism in England. By 1554, Protestant exiles were beginning to arrive in Geneva. The theological, social, and political situation in Geneva fostered extensive discussions about authority, tyranny, and resistance. In this context, the fact that Magdeburg was lifted up as an "outstanding example" to be emulated is significant. Many people not only followed Magdeburg's lead, they approved of this course of action

Beza's other tract, *On the Rights of Magistrates*, quotes *The Magdeburg Confession* in the title and is more interesting than *On the Punishment of Heretics*. *On the Rights of Magistrates* was written in response to the tragedy of the St. Bartholomew's Day Massacre (August 24, 1572) in which thousands of French Protestants were killed in and around Paris. Beza writes passionately and directly about the right and, echoing Magdeburg, the duty to resist. One striking aspect of this reference to the *Confession* is the historical context: Twenty-four years after the *Confession* was written, the event was still an "outstanding example" of justified resistance and the document remained a source for polemic.

Why was Magdeburg such a potent *exemplum*? The belief that inferior magistrates had a right to resist a tyrannical superior was, by 1574, quite common; this fundamental insight is not, then, the determinative factor. In fact, it may be argued that Martin Bucer's[3] *Explication of the Gospel of Matthew* was more influential in helping to develop the theory of resistance by lesser magistrates in Geneva than was *The Magdeburg Confession*. However, Bucer's writings remained merely theoretical. In Magdeburg, theory became practice.

Beza used the *Confession* as more than an example. He drew from some of its arguments to support and bolster his own position. He echoed Magdeburg's distinction between being a sole victim of injustice (which one must suffer patiently, even to martyrdom) and a magistrate charged with the protection of others. In the latter case, a magistrate must resist to protect his subjects. Beza also echoed the *Confession* in his discussion of the levels of injustice.

Similar to Magdeburg, in Beza's writings a magistrate is not permitted to resist simply because the ruler is unjust. He may only resist when the superior begins to coerce a lower magistrate into unjust and sinful acts. As in Magdeburg, the magistrate must refuse to obey *and* actively resist:

> But if the tyrant forbids what God commands, you should not at all judge that you have performed your duty if you have merely refused to obey the tyrant, unless at the same time you obey the command of God as we declared that Obadiah did, who not merely refrained from slaying the prophets of God, but even protected and nourished them in defiance of the command of Ahab and Jezebel, since the Lord bids us, each as far as his calling permits, to bring succor to his brethren in peril.[4]

This sense of a magistrate's responsibility to and for his subjects is a hallmark of *The Magdeburg Confession*. As in the *Confession*, the lesser magistrate is not excused from his responsibility because of the injustice of a superior. In fact, his responsibility to protect his subjects is increased. Beza notes these additional rights and responsibilities of the magistracy. In the *Confession* of 1550, in keeping with its Lutheran character, the magistracy is part of God's order in creation. Therefore, God establishes the magistracy. In Beza, God also establishes the magistracy. The perspective is, however, quite different; while the Magdeburg pastors followed Luther and viewed government through the lenses of the two kingdoms, Beza understands government largely in terms of covenant. He emphasizes the establishment of the government *by the governed*. In a covenant between

God and the people, a leader is chosen for the people, not the people for a leader. In the selection of Saul as king of Israel, Beza affirmed, God only anointed Saul after the people had urged God to provide them with a king. This covenantal understanding of authority was not possible within the framework of *The Magdeburg Confession* because of Luther's reluctance to embrace covenantal theology. *The Magdeburg Confession* did play a significant role in the development of Beza's theory, as did other streams of thought.

John Knox (c. 1513–72) was the principal reformer in Scotland. He began his career as a Catholic priest but became a Protestant around 1543. He preached in Saint Andrews, Scotland, until he was taken prisoner by the French in 1547. Freed two years later, Knox became a chaplain in the court of Edward VI. When Edward died in 1553, Knox became one of the first Marian exiles to flee to Geneva.

In Geneva, Knox changed his mind concerning a Christian's absolute obligation to submit to the government.[5] He also most likely encountered *The Magdeburg Confession* for the first time. It is impossible to decide whether the *Confession* played a role in changing his mind or the political situation in England precipitated this change. Yet for the rest of Knox's literary and ecclesial career, the *Confession* played a significant role in his understanding of resistance to tyranny.

In 1564, in a debate over the continuation of the Roman Mass under Queen Mary of Scotland, Knox referred to and quoted from *The Magdeburg Confession*:

> He presented unto the secretary the *Apology* of Magdeburg, and willed him to read the names of the ministers who had subscribed the defense of the town to a most just defense and then added, "That to resist a tyrant is not to resist God, nor yet his ordinance."[6]

This quotation reflects a transition in Knox's theological perspective as well as in his understanding of resistance. The first transition is his interpretation of Rom 13:1. In general, Paul's statement proved to be the stumbling block to resistance theories in the medieval church. At Magdeburg, the stumbling block was re-framed as an *aid* to resistance. Scholars have noted that this modification in the understanding of Romans 13 is the key difference between more conservative understandings of resistance in the 1530s and 1540s and the "Radical Calvinist" understanding of resistance developed in the 1550s, 1560s, and 1570s. However, this transition began in Magdeburg.[7] Knox clearly echoes Magdeburg in his reinterpretation of Romans:

> True it is, God has commanded kings to be obeyed; but likewise true it is, that in things which they commit against his glory or when cruelly without cause they rage against their brethren, the members of Christ's body he has commanded no obedience, but rather he has approved, yea, and greatly rewarded, such as have opposed themselves to their ungodly commandments and blind rage . . .[8]

This shift in the understanding of Romans continued to play an important role in the theories of resistance put forth by Bishop John Ponet[9] and Christopher Goodman. John Knox also reflected Magdeburg in his understanding of the source and authority of lesser magistrates. Unlike Beza, who looked to the people as one source for the ruler's authority, Knox understood that God had established the magistracy for the benefit of the people. Thus, the ruler does not owe the people justice, but the king must act justly because God has commanded it.

Like Beza, Knox also was influenced by others. He clearly went beyond the *Confession* in advocating an active role for the magistrate in establishing "true religion" and stamping out "idolatry." Yet at many key points Knox drew heavily from the Lutheran tradition reflected in Magdeburg.

The *Confession* continued to have an effect throughout the 16th century. Johann Sleiden in his *The State of Religion and the Commonwealth* (a history of the Reformation and the Schmalkaldic Wars written in 1555) referred to the *Confession* in quite positive terms.[10] *The State of Religion and the Commonwealth* was translated into English by 1560 and republished again in 1689. Robert Kingdon has noted the continuing influence of the *Confession* in the Netherlands during the 16th and into the 17th centuries. In short, we can clearly say that the *Confession* in Magdeburg continued to have an impact well into the early Modern Era.

BONHOEFFER'S BOW TO MAGDEBURG

At about 4 P.M. on April 5, 1943, the Gestapo arrested Dietrich Bonhoeffer for participating in a conspiracy to overthrow or assassinate Adolf Hitler. *Abwehr* (counterintelligence) chief Admiral Canaris led this conspiracy. Two years later, on April 9, 1945, at the Flossenburg concentration camp, Bonhoeffer, together with Canaris and others, was hanged.

Within months, Bishop George Bell of Chichester, England, declared Bonhoeffer a martyr for the faith. (To this day, the Anglican communion celebrates April 9 as an anniversary of Bonhoeffer's martyrdom; in 1998, a statue of Bonhoeffer was dedicated in Westminster Abbey as part of a memorial to martyrs.) Later, the pastors of Bielefeld appealed to Bonhoeffer's father and asked him to urge cities not to name streets after his son. They argued that he was a martyr to the faith, not a participant in political resistance. Karl Bonhoeffer rejected their plea. Today, in the museum that sits in the middle of what once was the Prinz-Albrecht Strasse Prison, Bonhoeffer's picture is the first picture one sees. He is recorded there as a Lutheran pastor who participated in the resistance to Hitler. Was he a martyr for his faith or a political conspirator?

Bonhoeffer was raised within a traditional Lutheran home. During his theological training, however, he was greatly influenced by Karl Barth, the leading Calvinist theologian of that era. Eberhard Bethge records that Bonhoeffer's resistance was theologically and ethically motivated. Was Bonhoeffer's action influenced by Barth (and, therefore, Calvin), by Luther, or perhaps by both?

A number of scholars, both in America and Germany, suggest that Dietrich Bonhoeffer was a traditional Lutheran but an operational Barthian. Yet Uwe Siemon-Netto has argued that Bonhoeffer was a traditional Lutheran and, in fact, a Gnesio-Lutheran. Siemon-Netto briefly notes a connection between Matthias Flacius and Bonhoeffer. Bonhoeffer's cousin, Christoph von Hase, wrote a biography of Flacius in 1940. Bonhoeffer and von Hase were not just cousins they were also close confidants and intellectual comrades-in-arms. What must be examined further is the degree to which Flacius and the events of Magdeburg in 1550 affected Bonhoeffer. In his book, von Hase writes:

> The confusion in the evangelical camp was great. However, as a true pupil of Luther's there surfaced Matthias Flacius, who with unbending courage defended the freedom of the Lutheran faith against all papal might and who coined the term *casus confessionis* to describe the situation. . . . Let us in our time prove, as did the Magdeburgers in their day, "that there are minds who love God's word, their fatherland, and their freedom."[11]

Did Bonhoeffer follow the pastors of Magdeburg? While Bonhoeffer was deeply influenced by Barth on many levels, his actions during World War II may reflect not Barth, but Luther. The import of this link is further to deflate the prevalent notion that Luther engendered only a quietist response to authoritarianism and that one should seek another explanation when a Lutheran resister is found. A connection between Magdeburg and Bonhoeffer would also demonstrate the influence of Magdeburg in political and theological discourse beyond the 16th century. The 16th-century connections are vital, but a direct connection to contemporary theology would also demonstrate the lasting influence of the Magdeburg pastors.

POLITICS OF THE FAITHFUL

In many ways politics and religion function similarly in our lives. They provide us with frames of reference, social structures, mores, and roots. They help us to define who we are. Because they function similarly, it is sometimes easy to blur the lines of separation or demarcation. Those lines are important because of the major fundamental difference between politics and religion. The former deals with penultimate issues, the latter in the world of ultimacy and eternity.

Politics is about people. It is about how people interact, how they acquire what they need, how they dispense justice, how they maintain order. The currency of politics is conflict and then—one hopes—confluence or compromise. Conflict emerges over resources and values. We do not have an infinite supply of resources, so we must make decisions about how resources are collected, used, and allocated. We also do not have a uniform set of beliefs about the type of society that we wish for our families and ourselves, so decisions must be made between conflicting mores or values. The process by which these decisions are made is the realm of politics.[12]

Government is the structure by which those decisions become a reality. Government is about power. Governments can be established by brute force, the consent of the masses, or anything in between.[13] Government has institutions that regulate life through influence and coercive force, for example, armies, penal codes, police forces, etc. The coercive nature of government and its connection to politics is what makes mingling politics with religion so dangerous.

The Gospel and Christian faith concern salvation. The questions that confronted Luther continue to confront people today: "How do I know that God loves me?" "How do I know that God accepts me?" Transcendence is the first currency of Christian vocabulary. Yet Christianity also has an important immanent nature. Christian faith is not simply about a saving relationship to Jesus Christ. It also concerns one's relationship to one's neighbors. Faith active in love (the liturgy after the liturgy) has been an important aspect of Christian theology since its earliest days when provisions were made for the well-being of widows and orphans. This aspect of Christian social ethics was also a hallmark of Luther's theology:

Now there is no greater service of God than Christian love which helps and serves the needy, as Christ himself will judge and testify at the Last Day, Matthew 25 [:31–46].[14]

In a similar fashion, politics is essentially immanent, but it also has transcendent qualities. It builds structures and institutions not for personal gain, but for the betterment of the community's present and future. In this light, it is easy to see how the lines between religion and politics can sometimes become blurred. Here Luther's distinction is critical. The *penultimate* nature of government was important to Luther because it ensured that human beings could not reify particular political concepts. Reification grants to political questions a quality they have not been given by God and do not deserve. To absolutize political structures and ideologies often leads to demonization of opponents and undermines the pragmatic nature of politics and governance.

Luther did not advocate a general theory of resistance. Yet the success of Magdeburg in 1550–51 demonstrates that it is historically inaccurate to attribute political quietism to Luther, either negatively as in Troeltsch (Luther did not have a theory of resistance) or positively as in Barth (Luther's two kingdoms necessitated quietism). The resistance affirmed by the Magdeburg pastors was clearly based in Luther. Luther's political legacy is not, and cannot, be the cause of much 20th-century tragedy. Luther's legacy, more properly, belongs to the city of Magdeburg and all those who found in these faithful pastors and laypersons an example of conviction and courage for the sake of the Gospel.

ABBREVIATIONS

ARG   *Archive for Reformation History/Archiv für Reformationsgeschichte*

Confession   *Bekentnis Unterricht und Vermanung der Pfarrherrn und Prediger der Christlichen Kirchen zu Magdeburgk (1550).* (The *Confession* is numbered by signature leaves. Each leaf is assigned a letter and a number. Only one side of a leaf is numbered; the other side is blank. When citing, the numbered side is labeled *r* for *recto;* the back is labeled *v* for *verso.* Thus, A1v refers to the first signature, the first leaf, back side.)

CWTM   *The Collected Works of Thomas Müntzer.* Edited and translated by Peter Matheson. Edinburgh: T & T Clark, 1998.

CTQ   *Concordia Theological Quarterly*

Enc   *Encounter*

Int   *Interpretation*

JES   *Journal of Ecumenical Studies*

JHI   *Journal of the History of Ideas*

KJV   King James Version of the Bible

LQ   *Lutheran Quarterly*

LW   *Luther's Works.* American Edition. General editors Jaroslav Pelikan and Helmut T. Lehmann. 56 vols. St. Louis: Concordia, and Muhlenberg and Philadelphia: Fortress, 1955–86.

NRSV   New Revised Standard Version of the Bible

SCJ   *Sixteenth Century Journal*

WA   *D. Martin Luthers Werke. Kritische Gesamtausgabe.* 68 vols. Weimar: Hermann Böhlaus Nachfolger, 1883–1999.

WABr   *D. Martin Luthers Werke. Kritische Gesamtausgabe. Briefwechsel.* 18 vols. Weimar: Hermann Böhlaus Nachfolger, 1930–85.

WATr   *D. Martin Luthers Werke: Kritische Gesamtausgabe. Tischreden.* 6 vols. Weimar: Hermann Böhlaus Nachfolger, 1912–21. Reprinted in 2000. (References in text are to volume, page, then talk number. Thus 4:239, no. 4342 = volume 4, page 239, Table Talk number 4342.)

WABi   *D. Martin Luthers Werke. Kritische Gesamtausgabe. Die Deutsche Bibel.* 12 vols in 15. Weimar: Hermann Böhlaus Nachfolger, 1906–61.

NOTES

PREFACE

[1] For example, as we will note in chapter 4, siding against the emperor in the late 1540s was the least likely avenue Magdeburg could follow to achieve its political goals. More often than not, siding against Charles V led to a death sentence and not freedom.

[2] The critical editions of Luther's writings are first—in German and Latin—*D. Martin Luthers Werke, Kritische Gesamtausgabe*, 107 vols. (Weimar: Hermann Böhlaus Nachfolger, 1883–1999); and second—in English—*Luther's Works*, American Edition, 56 vols. (St. Louis: Concordia, and Muhlenberg and Philadelphia: Fortress, 1955–86). Critical editions of Luther's major political writings and biblical commentaries exist in English and are readily available to the interested reader. Whenever possible, I have referred to the English *Luther's Works*; translations from WA are my own.

CHAPTER 1: CHRISTIAN IDENTITY AND POLITICAL IDENTITY

[1] Carter Lindberg, *The European Reformations* (Oxford: Blackwell, 1996), 2.

[2] Emile Durkheim, *The Elementary Forms of Religious Life* (New York: Free Press, 1965), 47: Religion is "the unified system of belief and practices relative to sacred things, that is, things that are set apart and forbidden, beliefs and practices which unite into one single moral community . . . all those who adhere to them."

[3] Peter Berger, *The Sacred Canopy: Elements of a Sociological Theory of Religion* (Garden City: Doubleday, 1969), 6.

[4] Berger, *Sacred Canopy*, 8.

[5] Roland Bainton, *Here I Stand: A Life of Martin Luther* (New York: Abingdon-Cokesbury, 1950), 33: "Luther knew perfectly well why youths should make themselves old and nobles make themselves abased. This life is only a brief period of training for the life to come, where the saved will enjoy an eternity of bliss and the damned will suffer everlasting torment. With their eyes they will behold the despair which can never experience the mercy of extinction. With their ears they will hear the moans of the damned. They will inhale sulphurous fumes and writhe in incandescent but unconsuming flame. All this will last forever and forever and forever. These were the ideas on which Luther had been nurtured."

[6] Later Luther described the weight of this angst or foreboding in his *Explanations of the Ninety-Five Theses*, LW 31:129f.: "I myself 'knew a man' [2 Cor 12:2] who

claimed that he had often suffered these punishments, in fact, over a very brief period of time. Yet they were so great and so much like hell that no tongue could adequately express them, no pen could describe them, and one who had not himself experienced them could not believe them. And so great were they that, if they had been sustained or had lasted for half an hour, even for one tenth of an hour, he would have perished completely and all of his bones would have been reduced to ashes. At such a time God seems terribly angry, and with him the whole creation. At such a time there is no flight, no comfort, within or without, but all things accuse."

[7] Martin Brecht, *Martin Luther: Shaping and Defining the Reformation, 1521–1532* (trans. James L. Schaaf; Philadelphia: Fortress, 1990), 49: "He left his parents and relatives against their wishes, taking up the cowl and monastic life in the conviction that this sort of life and its rigorous activity would be rendering great obedience to God. Perhaps in this way Luther was seeking a solution for the problems confronting him. Certainly the withdrawal from the world was not an end in itself. It was done in order to become truly pious, to serve and obey God, something that could occur in a special way in a monastery. The reason for this service, however, was the concern for salvation of one's soul. 'I took the vow for the sake of my salvation. [LW 54:338]' "

[8] Lindberg, *Reformations*, 64: "Between the six worship services of each day which began at 2:00 A.M., Luther sandwiched intense prayer, meditation, and spiritual exercises. But this was just the normal routine, which Luther in his zeal to mortify his flesh and make himself acceptable to God soon surpassed. 'I tortured myself with prayers, fasting, vigils and freezing; the frost alone might have killed me.' (LW 24:24) It has been suggested that his long periods of fasting, self-flagellation, and sleepless nights in a stone cell without a blanket all contributed to the continual illness that plagued him for the rest of his life. Later in life, Luther remarked: 'I almost fasted myself to death, for again and again I went for three days without taking a drop of water or a morsel of food. I was very serious about it.' (LW 54:339–40)."

[9] Martin Luther, *Lectures on Galatians*, LW 27:13.

[10] Bainton, *Here I Stand*, 54.

[11] WA 58 I:27. Quoted in Timothy George, *Theology of the Reformers* (Nashville: Broadman, 1988), 63.

[12] Bainton, *Here I Stand*, 60. This makes reference to the dramatic conversion experience of Saul of Tarsus in the book of Acts.

[13] WA 55:6.

[14] See Matt 27:46 and Mark 15:34.

[15] Ps 22:1a.

[16] See Anselm, Archbishop of Canterbury, *Cur Deus Homo: Why God Became Man, and The Virgin Conception and Original Sin* (trans, intro., and notes by Joseph M. Colleran; Albany: Magi Books, 1969).

[17] Thomas Aquinas, *Summa Theologia* (trans. and comments by T. C. O'Brien O. P.; New York: Black Friars in conjunction with McGraw Hill, 1965), IIIa, 46; IIIa, 48,6; IIIa, 49,1.

[18] See 2 Cor 5:21: "For our sake he made him to be sin who knew no sin, so that in him we might become the righteousness of God."

[19] Bainton, *Here I Stand*, 63.

[20] LW 54:194.

[21] Heiko Oberman, *Luther: Man between God and the Devil* (trans. Eileen Walliser-Schwarzbart; New York: Image Books, Doubleday, 1982), 155.

[22] LW 34:336f, *emphasis added.*

[23] See *On the Revolutions of the Heavenly Spheres*, 1543.

[24] See Philip S. Watson, *Let God Be God: An Interpretation of the Theology of Martin Luther* (London: Epworth Press, 1947), 33ff.

[25] See Martin Luther, "Heidelberg Disputation," no. 20, LW 31:41: "He deserves to be called a theologian, however, who comprehends the visible and manifest things of God seen through suffering and the cross."

[26] See George, *Reformers*, 58: "For Luther, in the realm of true theology reason functioned only *ex post facto*, that is, as an ordering principle by which the biblical revelation was clearly set forth. Enlightened reason, reason which was incorporated into faith could thus 'serve faith in thinking about something,' for reason informed by the Holy Spirit 'takes all things from the Word.' "

[27] See Luther, "Heidelberg Disputation," LW 31:41: "He who wishes to philosophize by using Aristotle without danger to his soul must first become thoroughly foolish in Christ." Also see Martin Luther, *Disputation Against Scholastic Theology*, theses 47–49, LW 31:12, where Luther attacks the rampant speculation of the scholastics and the idea that even the inner Trinitarian life can be proved by syllogism!

[28] "The word of God endures forever"; "*des Herrn Wort bleibt in Ewigkeit*" (Martin Luther, WABi). This phrase "was adopted as [a] motto by Luther's sovereign, Frederick the Wise, and his successors. The original 'Protestant' princes walking out of the imperial Diet of Speyer 1529, unruly peasants following Thomas Müntzer, and from 1531 to 1547 the coins, medals, flags, and guns of the Schmalkaldic League all bore the most famous Reformation slogan, the first Evangelical confession: the Word of the Lord remains forever" quoted from the inside jacket of *Lutheran Quarterly*.

[29] Martin Luther, "Preface to the Old Testament (1545)," LW 35:236.

[30] See Luther, "Heidelberg Disputation," no. 20, LW 31.

[31] Alister E. McGrath, *Luther's Theology of the Cross* (Oxford: Basil Blackwell, 1985), 150.

[32] See theses 3 and 4 of Luther's "Heidelberg Disputation." Jos E. Vercruyse in "Gesetz und Liebe, Die Struktur der 'Heidelberg Disputation' Luthers [1518]," *Lutherjahrbuch* 48 (1981): 11–12, vividly demonstrates this dichotomy by placing the two theses side by side:

3. The Works of Human	4. The Works of God
Always look splendid	Always look deformed
Appear to be good	Appear to be bad
Are nevertheless in all probability mortal sins	Are nevertheless in very truth immortal merits

[33] Kenneth Hagan, "The Testament of a Worm: Luther on Testament to 1525," *Consensus* 8.1 (1982): 16f: "Luther's understanding and experience of covenants, historical and contemporary, seem to be consistently negative because they circumscribe freedom—theologically, the freedom of God. 'If' type soteriologies are the

way of the Law. The freedom of the Christian man depends on the sovereign freedom of God to give the promise of the New Testament."

[34] Heb 9:12–17.

[35] Martin Luther, *The Freedom of a Christian* (1520), LW 31:355: "Thus Christ has made it possible for us, provided we believe in him, to be not only his brethren, co-heirs, and fellow-kings, but also his fellow priests. Therefore we may boldly come into the presence of God in the spirit of faith [Heb 10:19, 22] and cry 'Abba, Father!' . . ."

[36] Luther, *The Freedom of a Christian* (1520), LW 31:373: "Our faith in Christ does not free us from works but from false opinions concerning works, that is, from the foolish presumption that justification is acquired by works. Faith redeems, corrects, and preserves our consciences so that we know that righteousness does not consist in works . . ."

[37] Carter Lindberg, "Justification by Faith Alone: *The* Lutheran Proposal to the Churches," *New Conversations* 10.2 (1988): 37.

[38] See Martin Luther, "Two Types of Righteousness" (1519), LW 31:297–306; and Martin Luther, *Bondage of the Will* (1525), LW 33:15–295.

[39] George, *Reformers*, 56.

[40] WA 7:502: "Nearly the entire Scripture and all knowledge of theology depend upon the correct understanding of Law and Gospel."

[41] It is this aspect of limiting evil and encumbering chaos that Luther will look to when confronted with a call by various magistrates for a justification of resistance to the emperor.

[42] Watson, *Let God Be God*, 155.

[43] Martin Luther, *Concerning the Letter and the Spirit* (1521), LW 39:186: "Therefore it is impossible for someone who does not first hear the Law and let himself be killed by the letter to hear the Gospel and let the grace of the Spirit bring him to life. Grace is only given to those who long for it. Life is a help only to those who are dead, grace only to sin, the Spirit only to the letter."

[44] Martin Luther, *Bondage of the Will* (1525), LW 33:261.

[45] Deut 5:17 KJV.

[46] Rom 8:1.

[47] Gerhard Forde, "Law and Gospel in Luther's Hermeneutic," *Int* 37 (1983): 241.

[48] Note that in the Sermon on the Mount, Jesus expands the requirements of the righteous from acts to thoughts, e.g., "You have heard that it was said to those of ancient times, 'You shall not murder'; and 'whoever murders shall be liable to judgment.' But I say to you that if you are angry with a brother or sister, you will be liable to judgment; and if you insult a brother or sister, you will be liable to the council; and if you say, 'You fool,' you will be liable to the hell of fire" (Matt 5:21–22).

[49] Ralph Keen, *Divine and Human Authority in Reformation Thought: German Theologians on Political Order, 1520–1555* (Nieuwkoop, Netherlands: B. de Graaf, 1997).

[50] Luther and John Calvin are both often labeled magisterial reformers because they relate to the magistracy of their region and share a common view on the validity of secular authority. However, Calvin's theory of political authority bears much more resemblance to the *corpus christianum* of Leo than it does to Luther.

[51] Luther, *The Freedom of a Christian* (1520), LW 31:343: "A Christian is a perfectly free lord of all, subject to none. A Christian is perfectly dutiful servant of all, subject to all."

[52] Martin Luther, *To the Christian Nobility of the German Nation* (1520), LW 44:127–29 passim.

[53] Luther, *Temporal Authority* (1523), LW 45:105: "The temporal government has laws which extend no further than to life and property and external affairs on earth, for God cannot and will not permit anyone but himself to rule over the soul."

[54] Luther, *Temporal Authority* (1523), LW 45:91: "[God] has subjected [the wicked] to the sword so that, even though they would like to, they are unable to practice their wickedness, and if they do practice it they cannot do so without fear or with success and impunity."

[55] See Luther, *Temporal Authority* (1523), LW 45:109. Luther notes that neither kings nor bishops are doing their jobs well because they seem so obsessed with doing the work of the other.

[56] In *Temporal Authority* (1523), LW 45, Luther makes this allusion. It is both humorous and poignant. It is humorous because Luther prescribes a common remedy for insanity to those who confuse the two, poignant because of the cities he chose. "Leipzig was the capital of Albertine Saxony, ruled by the hostile Duke George the Bearded from 1500–1539, while Wittenberg was the capital of Ernestine Saxony, ruled by the friendly Elector Frederick the Wise from 1486–1525" (LW 45:107, n. 56).

[57] Luther, *Temporal Authority* (1523), LW 45:105.

[58] Luther, *Temporal Authority* (1523), LW 45:91.

[59] Carter Lindberg, "Theology and Politics: Luther the Radical and Müntzer the Reactionary," *Enc* 37.4 (1976): 361.

[60] Randall C. Zachman, *The Assurance of Faith: Conscience in the Theology of Martin Luther and John Calvin* (Minneapolis: Fortress, 1993), 73.

[61] Lindberg, "Theology and Politics," 364.

[62] WA 27:417–18, quoted in Lindberg, "Theology and Politics," 364.

[63] Walter von Loewenich, *Luthers theologia crucis* (5th ed.; Wittenberg: Luther-Verlag, 1967), 79: "It was, in fact, Luther's view to the end of his life that faith and experience are often mutually exclusive. Seeing and believing stand in sharp contrast."

CHAPTER 2: THEORY BECOMES PRAXIS

[1] While, on the one hand, Einstein's theories of general and special relativity have given the world great benefits (e.g., the National Aeronautics and Space Administration space program, nuclear medicine for cancer treatment, field theory mechanics, black hole astronomy, etc.), they also have ushered in an era of untold suffering and fear (e.g., Hiroshima and Nagasaki, Mutual Assured Destruction, International Continental Ballistic Missiles). Luther's revolution, likewise, produced its specific benefits and nightmares.

[2] See Steven Ozment, *Protestants: The Birth of a Revolution* (New York: Doubleday, 1992); also see chapter 4 in Carter Lindberg, *The European Reformations* (Oxford: Blackwell, 1996) and *Beyond Charity: Reformation Initiatives for the Poor* (Minneapolis: Fortress, 1993).

[3] Carter Lindberg, "Conflicting Models of Ministry: Luther, Karlstadt, and Müntzer," *CTQ* 41.4 (1977): 37.

[4] Peter Blickle, in *The Revolution of 1525: The German Peasants' War from a New Perspective* (trans. Thomas A. Brady Jr. & H. C. Erik Midelfort; Baltimore: Johns Hopkins University Press, 1981), makes a convincing argument for describing the events of 1525 as a revolution and the participants as more than just the peasants. For the sake of this chapter and the argument here, I shall continue to use the less accurate but more recognizable term *Peasants' War* and refer to the participants as *peasants*.

[5] James M. Stayer, *The German Peasants War and Anabaptist Community of Goods* (Montreal: McGill-Queen's University Press, 1991), 21.

[6] For a comprehensive introduction to modern historiography concerning the so-called Peasants' War, see Stayer, *German Peasants' War*, chapter 1.

[7] See *The Twelve Articles of Upper Swabia* in *Quellen zur Geschichte des Bauernkrieges* (ed. Günther Franz; Darmstadt, 1963), 174–79. Reprinted in Tom Scott and Bob Scribner, eds., *The German Peasants' War: A History in Documents* (Atlantic Highlands: Humanities Press, 1991), 252–57.

[8] Lindberg, *Reformations*, 164.

[9] Blickle, *Revolution of 1525*, 18.

[10] Pfeiffer had his own difficulties in reforming the church in Mühlhausen. In August 1523, he was banished. But by 1524, he had returned and solidified his position.

[11] Scott and Scribner, *German Peasants' War*, 37.

[12] See Eric W. Gritsch, *Thomas Muentzer: A Tragedy of Errors* (Minneapolis: Fortress, 1989), 143. He quotes a letter from Frederick to his brother John: "If it is the will of God, the common man will rule; if it is not . . . things will change. Let us beg God for forgiveness of our sins and leave it up to him."

[13] WABr 3:472. It is important to note that Luther had severe reservations about Müntzer's theology and aspirations for quite some time. As early as 1521, during Müntzer's time in Zwickau, differences between him and Luther are apparent. By February 1523, Luther seems to have made his reservations about Müntzer public. See Martin Brecht, *Martin Luther II: Shaping and Defining the Reformation, 1521–1532* (trans. James L. Schaaf; Philadelphia: Fortress, 1990), 147ff.

[14] Deut 7:1–5.

[15] CWTM, 140ff.

[16] Martin Luther, *Against the Robbing and Murdering Hordes of Peasants*, LW 46:50: "they are starting a rebellion, and are violently robbing and plundering monasteries and castles which are not theirs. . . . [R]ebellion is not just simple murder it is like a great fire which attacks and devastates the whole land. Thus rebellion brings with it a land filled with murder and bloodshed, it makes widows and orphans, and turns everything upside down, like the worst disaster. Therefore let anyone who can, smite, slay, stab, secretly or openly remembering that nothing is more poisonous, hurtful, or Devilish than a rebel. It is just as when one must kill a mad dog; if you do not strike him, he will strike you, and the whole land with you."

[17] CWTM, 144.

[18] Müntzer continued to use the phrase "in the field" in many letters throughout the rest of the campaign.

[19] Judges 6–7.

[20] CWTM, 155f.

[21] In this passage, God speaks to Gideon: "Then the LORD said to Gideon, 'With the three hundred that lapped I will deliver you, and give the Midianites into your hand. Let all the others go to their homes.' "

[22] Rom 2:9: "There will be anguish and distress for everyone who does evil."

[23] Dan 7:27: "The kingship and dominion and the greatness of the kingdoms under the whole heaven shall be given to the people of the holy ones of the Most High; their kingdom shall be an everlasting kingdom, and all dominions shall serve and obey them."

[24] CWTM, 156f.

[25] Scott and Scribner, "The Account [Confession] of Hans Hut, 26 November 1527," in German Peasants' War, 290. (Because I was curious about the phenomenon that Hut describes, I e-mailed a friend who is a meteorologist. He wrote back, "That optical phenomena can form when there are some very fine high, wispy cirrus clouds in the air. The sunlight can be refracted in such a way to cause a rainbow-like appearance to be present. In fact, this can happen quite often in a part of the sky on a mostly sunny day with some high cirrus clouds around.")

[26] Eric W. Gritsch, Reformer without a Church: The Life and Thought of Thomas Muentzer 1488?–1525 (Philadelphia: Fortress), 149.

[27] Scott and Scribner, "Count Phillip von Solms's report to his son Reinhard, 16 May 1525," in German Peasants' War, 290f.

[28] For an introduction into the labyrinth of research and controversy surrounding Müntzer and Müntzer scholarship, see Carter Lindberg, "Müntzeriana, A Review Essay," LQ 4.3 (Summer 1990), 195–214. For primary documents in English, see CWTM. For an examination of Müntzer and Müntzer scholarship, see Gritsch, Thomas Muentzer. For information on the early life and influences of Müntzer, see Ulrich Bubenheimer, Thomas Müntzer: Herkunft und Bildung (Leiden: E. J. Brill, 1989).

[29] Gritsch, Reformer, 1.

[30] George Lindbeck, The Nature of Doctrine (Philadelphia: Westminster, 1984), 16.

[31] Lindbeck, Nature of Doctrine, 16.

[32] Thomas Müntzer, "An Open Letter to the Brothers at Stolberg," (July 18, 1523): "The true Kingdom of God begins with genuine pleasure when the elect first see what God lets them discover in themselves, through His action, in the experience of the Spirit"; quoted in Michael G. Baylor, "Thomas Müntzer's First Publication," SCJ 17.4 (1989): 456.

[33] This is in keeping with Luther's general reluctance to mix the two kingdoms. Luther's doctrine of the two kingdoms held that one should act only within the arena of one's competency. As a theologian, Luther could only speak on whether something was sinful, not on whether something was legal. Thus, Luther distanced himself from politics in a measure that was not present in Müntzer.

[34] CWTM, 247f.

[35] Matt 7:19: "Every tree that does not bear good fruit is cut down and thrown into the fire." John 15:2, 6: "He removes every branch in me that bears no fruit. Every branch that bears fruit he prunes to make it bear more fruit. . . . Whoever does not

abide in me is thrown away like a branch and withers; such branches are gathered, thrown into the fire, and burned."

[36] Deut 13:5: "But those prophets or those who divine by dreams shall be put to death for having spoken treason against the LORD your God—who brought you out of the land of Egypt and redeemed you from the house of slavery—to turn you from the way in which the LORD your God commanded you to walk. So you shall purge the evil from your midst."

[37] CWTM, 244f.

[38] Rom 13:4: "But if you do what is wrong, you should be afraid, for the authority does not bear the sword in vain! It is the servant of God to execute wrath on the wrongdoer."

[39] Dan 7:24–27.

[40] CWTM, 250.

[41] For an enlightening survey of this connection, see William R. Stevenson Jr., *Sovereign Grace: The Place and Significance of Christian Freedom in John Calvin's Political Thought* (Oxford: Oxford University Press, 2000).

[42] Uwe Siemon-Netto, *The Fabricated Luther: The Rise and Fall of the Shirer Myth* (St. Louis: Concordia, 1995).

[43] Martin Luther, *Dr. Martin Luther's Warning to His Dear German People* (1531), LW 47:6.

[44] The *Augsburg Confession* itself became important later in *The Magdeburg Confession*.

[45] Erwin Iserloh, "The Imperial Diet of Augsburg," in *Reformation and Counter Reformation* (ed. Hubert Jedin and John Dolan; trans. Anselm Briggs and Peter W. Becker; vol. 10 of *The History of the Church*; New York: The Seabury Press, 1975), 260.

[46] W. D. J. Cargill Thompson, "Luther and the Right of Resistance to the Emperor," in *Church, Society, and Politics* (ed. Derek Baker; Oxford: Basil Blackwell for The Ecclesiastical History Society, 1975), 186 passim.

[47] Luther, *Warning*, LW 47:8.

[48] Mark U. Edwards Jr., *Luther's Last Battles: Politics and Polemics, 1531–46* (Ithaca: Cornell University Press, 1983), 25.

[49] Cynthia Grant Shoenberger, "Luther and the Justifiability of Resistance to Legitimate Authority," *JHI* 40 (1979): 11.

[50] W. D. J. Cargill Thompson, *The Political Thought of Martin Luther* (ed. Philip Broadhead; Totowa: Barnes & Noble Books, 1984), 106.

[51] For example, Luther wrote that he is "speaking as though in a dream" (*Warning*, LW 47:13), or "I do not wish to spur any to war or rebellion or even self-defense but only to peace" (*Warning*, LW 47:55). An interesting historical side note is the explanation that Nikolaus von Amsdorf and the Magdeburg pastors give for Luther's ambiguity. They write:

> As for the reasons why Dr. Luther . . . gives rather obscure and downright conflicting advice, these reasons have been learned privately from him by some of his friends . . . The reason was he wanted to hold both parties in check. He did not want to say that justified resistance is unjust in order not to strengthen the Papists. He also did not want to praise it or call it just so

that the patience of goodhearted people might thereby flag in their endurance of great injustice from the enemies . . . (*Confession*, M3r.)

[52] Edwards, *Last Battles*, 25ff.

[53] Luther, *Warning*, LW 47:11.

[54] Edwards, *Last Battles*, 25.

[55] Luther, *Warning*, LW 47:15: "Even now, if I were to be murdered in such a papist and clerical uprising . . ."

[56] Luther, *Warning*, LW 47:17: "Consequently, since they wage war with a bad conscience for a blasphemous cause, good fortune and success cannot attend them."

[57] Luther, *Warning*, LW 47:19.

[58] The section contains quite a long defense of Charles V. Charles V is not the real enemy; it is the pope. Luther attempts to show that Charles is not to blame—it is all the papists around him. While Luther's aim is clear, the portrayal of the emperor remains less than flattering. He comes off as an unwitting aid to the antichrist.

[59] Luther, *Warning*, LW 47:46f. This section is interesting because Luther makes use of an aspect of his two kingdoms doctrine: that the political sphere is governed by reason. He recounts a discussion between Cochlaeus and Eck (two of the Roman delegation) in which Eck finds evidence for saint worship in the Old Testament and Cochlaeus argues against such a position. The point Luther drives home is that not only do the papists support the devil, but they cannot even get their stories straight and "for this you are [going] to war and fight, etc." The sarcasm is impossible to miss. Is it reasonable to go off to war based on such poor logic?

[60] See Thomas Müntzer, "*A Highly Provoked Defense and Answer Against the Spiritless, Soft-Living Flesh at Wittenberg, Which has Befouled Pitiable Christianity in Perverted Fashion by its Theft of Holy Scripture*," *Mennonite Quarterly Review* 38.1 (January 1964): 24–36.

[61] WA 39:41–42.

[62] See Luther, *Warning*, LW 47, and *Torgau Declaration* (1530), also LW 47.

[63] Luther, "Admonition to Peace: A Reply to the Twelve Articles of the Peasants in Swabia (1525)," LW 46:32.

[64] Carter Lindberg, "Luther's Critique of the Ecumenical Assumption that Doctrine Divides but Service Unites," *JES* 27 (1990): 691. It is important to remember that Luther's greatest issue with Müntzer was his mixing of the Gospel with a political program. In fact, Luther wrote the Saxon princes in July 1524 counseling forbearance concerning Müntzer as long as he stuck to preaching. Preaching is allowable, even if it is wrong. If the spirit of Müntzer's teaching is true, it will be of no harm. If it is not, then time will show its error. Luther urged the princes to focus on their own spirits. "If our spirit is right, then it will neither be afraid of him nor anyone else. Let the spirits collide and fight it out. If meanwhile some are led astray, all right, such is war" (LW 37:367). Again a year later, and just before things completely fell apart, Luther wrote in his "Admonition to Peace": "No ruler ought to prevent anyone from teaching and believing whatever they please, whether it is the gospel or lies" (LW 45:83).

[65] Shoenberger, "Luther and the Justifiability of Resistance," 19.

[66] See Martin Luther, "Letter to the Elector Frederick, 29 May 1523," LW 49:40: "I am able to write Your Electoral Grace that my mind and intention have never

been—nor are they even now—set on slandering anyone of high or low position, nor on writing, teaching, or preaching anything which could cause disturbance, disunity, or rebellion in the Holy Roman Empire, or could lead Christians into error. I have often written and preached harshly against these things. *However, my sole purpose from beginning to end has been and still is to write, teach, preach, do, and promote nothing else but that which serves, and is necessary and useful, the strengthening of God's Word and honor*" (emphasis added).

[67] See, for example, Martin Luther's letters to Frederick (1/13–19/1519, LW 48:103; 1/25/1521, LW 48:195; 5/29/1523, LW 49:35), to Charles V (4/28/1521, LW 48:203), to the papal legate Cardinal Cajetan (10/18/1518, LW 48:87), and to Pope Leo X (1/5 or 6/1519, LW 48:100).

[68] See, for example, Luther's letter to the Elector Frederick (3/7 or 8/1522, LW 48:395ff): "I am returning not out of contempt for the authority of the Imperial Majesty or of Your Electoral Grace, or of any other government. Human authority is not always to be obeyed, namely, when it undertakes against the commandments of God . . . I know that this stay is without Your Electoral Grace's knowledge or consent. Your Electoral Grace is lord only of earthly goods and bodies, but Christ is the also the Lord of souls. To these he has sent me and for this [purpose] he has raised me up."

[69] Cargill Thompson, "Right of Resistance," 188.

[70] See Lindberg, "Luther's Critique," 691: "Luther's fundamental doctrinal commitment to justification by grace alone informed his rejection of all expressions of the *corpus Christianum*, whether of the medieval papacy or of the 'radical' Reformers. . . ."

[71] Martin Luther, "Letter to Elector Frederick 5 March 1522," LW 48:391.

Chapter 3: The Context
of *The Magdeburg Confession*

[1] Theodore Beza, *De Haereticis a ciuili Magistratu puniendis Libellus, aduersus Martini Bellii farraginewm, & nouorum Academicorum sectam, Theodoro Beza Vezelio aucture* (Geneva: Olivia Roberti Stephani, 1554).

[2] [E.] David Willis-Watkins, "Calvin's Prophetic Reinterpretation of Kingship," in *Probing the Reformed Tradition: Historical Essays in Honor of Edward A. Dowey, Jr.* (Louisville: Westminster/John Knox, 1989), 127.

[3] See Robert M. Kingdon, "Was the Protestant Reformation a Revolution?: The Case of Geneva," in *Church, Society, and Politics* (ed. Derek Baker; vol. 12 of *Studies in Church History*; Oxford: B. Blackwell for The Ecclesiastical History Society, 1975), 215ff.

[4] John Calvin, *Institutes of the Christian Religion* (ed. John Baillie; trans. Ford Lewis Battles; vol. 20–21 of *The Library of Christian Classics*; Philadelphia: Westminster, 1960), IV.20.3., 1488, *emphasis added*.

[5] Calvin, *Institutes*, IV.20.3., 1488.

[6] Calvin, *Institutes*, IV.20.2., 1487.

[7] Beza, *De Haereticis*. Quoted in Robert M. Kingdon, "The First Expression of Theodore Beza's Political Ideas," *ARG* 46 (1955): 92.

[8] Theodore Beza, *Du droit des magistrats sur leurs subiets. Traitte tres-necessaire en ce*

temps, pour aduertir de leur deuoir, tant les Magistrats que les Subiets: publie par ceux de Magdebourg l'an M D L: & maintenant reueu & augmente de plusieurs raisons & exemples (n. p., 1574). His reference to *The Magdeburg Confession* in the title created confusion between his tract and the work of the Magdeburg pastors.

[9] For example, see the following in the *Confession*: "that dear man Dr. Martin Luther, like the third Elijah" (A2r); "from the beginning of our cause, Luther's teaching was firmly established as incontrovertible and irrefutable" (A3v); "the teaching of Luther, which is the teaching of Christ" (A4v); "the chosen instrument of God, Dr. Luther" (B1r); "that man of God, Dr. Martin Luther, of blessed memory" (G4v); "Other readers outside this city can find everything better and more fully expressed in Dr. Luther's writings and similar writings to which nothing we have said here is alien. We also hope that they will be understood in this sense" (H1r); "Whereas what we are now doing is only preserving pure and immaculate that sacred inheritance entrusted to us by God through that man of God, Dr. Martin Luther" (H1v).

[10] *Confession*, A3v.

[11] Charles V quoted in Erwin Iserloh, "The Imperial Diet of Augsburg," in *Reformation and Counter Reformation* (ed. Hubert Jedin and John Dolan; trans. Anselm Briggs and Peter W. Becker; vol. 10 of *The History of the Church*; New York: The Seabury Press, 1975), 286.

[12] Josef Benzing, *Lutherbibliographie: Verzeichnis der Gedruckten Schriften Martin Luthers bis zu dessen Tod* (Baden-Baden: Heitz, 1966), nos. 2908–24 with 2913a. Luther's *Warning* was published in Wittenberg (five printings), Strasbourg (one printing), Magdeburg (two printings), and Reutlingen (one printing) in 1531. In 1546 it was re-issued in Wittenberg (two printings), Augsburg (one printing), Nuremberg (four printings), Strasbourg (one printing), and Tübingen (one printing). Note that the *Warning* was published in a wider circle of cities and had just as many printings in 1546 as it did in 1531.

[13] Iserloh, "The Imperial Diet of Augsburg," 293.

[14] *Confession*, B1v: "However, there is a remnant of some few of lowly estate, including some even among the defectors, who are steadfast, pious Christians, who alongside us and with us hold fast to pure Christian doctrine untainted and immaculate of the stain and mark of the Pope, and they confess our dear Lord Christ like the thief beside Christ on the Cross. The Lord Christ stands at the Cross, and we stand with him."

[15] For example, in a letter to Spalatin (2/8/1523), Amsdorf argued that a prince was obliged to defend the Gospel: "*Aestimo auem principem, sed christianum in spiritu et veritate, non in corpore et ceremoniis, cui moventur bella evangelium, posse belligere, immo debere suos* vel alios defendere." Quoted in Heinz Scheible, *Das Widerstandsrecht als Problem der deutsche Protestanten 1523–1546* (Gütersloher: Verlagshaus Gerd Mohn, 1969), 19.

[16] Burkhart was murdered by a group of merchants. Burkhart was notorious for requisitioning work, then failing to pay for it when it was completed. For more information, see "Magdeburg Geschichte 1000–1500" at www.magdeburg-online.de or *Chronik der Stadt Magdeburg, ed. Oberbürgermeister der Stadt Magdeburg* (Berlin: Friedrich Ernst Hübsch Verlag, 1936).

[17] Oliver K. Olson, "Theology of Revolution: Magdeburg, 1550–1551," *SCJ* 3.1 (April 1972): 63.

[18] For example, see a letter written by the city council to the emperor's legate Lazarus Schwendi (July 1547) in Friedrich Wilhelm Hoffman, *Geschichte der Stadt*

Magdeburg, nach den Quellen bearbeitet, vol. 2 (Magdeburg: Baensch, 1847), 235ff: "[our] humble request that you permit us the pure saving divine Word, as it is preached here and in many places out of Grace to the honor of our dear God and our salvation and bliss, whereby we and all the believers—also the Lord to his Godly honor—could be happily preserved."

[19] For example, Elector John Frederick was stripped of his electoral dignity following his defeat, and both he and Landgrave Philip of Hesse were sentenced to death for their resistance to the emperor. In both cases, the death sentences were commuted; however, neither regained his original political authority.

[20] Olson, "Theology of Revolution," 66: "[T]he astonishing decision to continue resistance to the empire after the defeat of the Schmalkaldic League armies reveals something more than ordinary political calculation. In a letter to the Prince Elector during the black days of May 1547, the city council pledged to remain faithful to the Christlicher Verein. Magdeburg would obey the emperor only in secular matters, not in religious, and would not surrender."

[21] Dietrich Bonhoeffer picked up this slogan in response to the Deutsche Kirche's position that its Aryan bylaws were *adiaphora*.

[22] They note that their situation is similar to that which threatened Luther. They state: "At one time it seemed that it might perhaps be all over with him [Luther] and his whole doctrine, as it does again in our time" (*Confession*, A2–A3.)

[23] Olson, "Theology of Revolution," 70f.

[24] Oliver K. Olson, "Matthias Flacius Illyricus," in *Shapers of Religious Traditions in Germany, Switzerland, and Poland, 1560–1600* (ed. Jill Raitt; New Haven: Yale University Press, 1981), 4.

Chapter 4: *The Magdeburg Confession*

[1] For a survey of these documents, see Cynthia Grant Shoenberger, "The Confession of Magdeburg and the Lutheran Doctrine of Resistance" (Ph.D. diss., Columbia University, 1972).

[2] The *Confession* is 129 pages in length; the next longest treatise or tract, *Antwort*, which also was published in 1550, runs only 32 pages.

[3] The document concludes with a list of signatories that includes all the pastors of the city. While many other pastors had fled to the city because of the Interim, only clergy who were in fact pastors of city churches signed the document. The signers are numbered, but in what is an obvious anachronism, one cannot miss the similarity to the U. S. *Declaration of Independence* because there is one signature—unnumbered and quite a bit larger than the rest—that tops the list, that of Nikolaus von Amsdorf. The other signers are: "1. Niclas Han (Pastor to St. Ulrich's [church]), 2. Lucas Rosental (Church of St. Johannes), 3. Johannes Stengel (of St. Jacob), 4. Henning Freden (of St. Catherine), 5. Ambrosis Kitfeld (of St. Peter), 6. Johannes Baumbarten (of Holy Spirit), 7. Joachim Wolterstorff (South Fortress—die Sudenburg), 8. Heinrich Gercken (in the New City—newe Stadt.) All ministers signed in their own hand for themselves and their fellow servants" (*Confession*, Q3r).

[4] Oliver K . Olson, "Theology of Revolution: Magdeburg, 1550–1551," *SCJ* 3.1 (April 1972): 67, n. 49. The note accompanies the copy of the *Confession* in the collection of the Wolfenbüttel Library.

[5] At many times the text addresses Charles V in the second person.

[6] Ps 119:46: "Ich rede von deinen Zeugnissen vor Königen und schäme mich nicht" ("I will also speak of your decrees before kings, and shall not be put to shame").

[7] See 2 Sam 12:1–12. N.B., the same citation is on the title page of the *Augsburg Confession*. That is to say, the authors are self-consciously Lutheran.

[8] Desiderius Erasmus, *Annotations on Romans* (ed. Robert D. Sider; trans. and annotated by John B. Payne, Albert Rabil Jr., Robert D. Sider, and Warren S. Smith Jr.; vol. 56 of *Collected Works of Erasmus*; Toronto: University of Toronto Press, 1994), 350.

[9] WABi 7:69.

[10] Rom 13:3.

[11] Acts 9:4: "Saul, Saul, was verfolgst du mich? . . . Es wird dir schwer werden wider den Stachel lecken" ("Saul, Saul, why persecutest thou me? [it is] hard for thee to kick against the pricks" KJV). The second sentence in this quotation is no longer considered authoritative. In 1550, though, it was contained in both the *Vulgate* and Luther's translations of the Greek New Testament.

[12] *Confession*, A1v.

[13] With a touch of irony, the pastors at one point note that the emperor does not force Jews or "Mohammadins" to convert to "Popism." They ask why they cannot be afforded the same right (*Confession*, J1r).

[14] *Confession*, A3r.

[15] *Confession*, A3v. Here is another example of the difference between the Magdeburg pastors and Thomas Müntzer. For Müntzer, Luther's belief that "the Word did it all" was naïve and irresponsible. In fact, Müntzer took the same position that the emperor had taken: Religious hegemony must be compelled by force if necessary.

[16] *Confession*, A3v-A4r, *emphasis added*.

[17] *Confession*, A2r: "And to sum up: Surely all God's miraculous works are not to be entirely in vain, when Luther had a fortunate beginning to these enterprises for God, and even more fortunate continuation in them, and finally a most fortunate conclusion to these affairs; prevailing against all grim raving and raging of the world and the gates of hell? As God has adorned this prophet of his with many glorious testimonies and fortunate advancement in his calling, so to what now follows is to be considered not the least of these beneficent miracles."

[18] *Confession*, B1r: "We must also reflect that, in order to court the enemy, some people libelously slander the chosen instrument of God, Dr. Luther, through whose service God once again led us to such insight, and who liberated us from the Babylonian captivity of the Antichrist; and in addition they knowingly would subject true Christians to the Antichrist again. These examples and many more, as they in truth actually are, are nothing but a denial of the *Augsburg Confession* and with it, a denial too of Christ the Lord Himself."

[19] *Confession*, B2v-B3r.

[20] *Confession*, A1v.

[21] The lesser magistrate is obliged to defend his subjects against an unjust force seeking to subvert Christian teaching. However, this is not carte blanche. The lesser magistrate is only to defend his subjects. As an individual Christian man—alone, perhaps—he ought to suffer the injustice and leave vengeance to God. It is only in

his position as a magistrate that he is called on to act. See *Confession*, B2v.

[22] *Confession*, B2r: "We recognize our responsibility to the honor of God and for the consolation of the whole church, our responsibility namely to bear public witness to the oft-mentioned teaching of the Holy Gospel revealed anew to us through Dr. Martin Luther, and to bear testimony to the *Augsburg Confession.*"

[23] The *Confession*'s summary of doctrine touches on: (1) the nature of the Trinity; (2) creation, the Fall, and sin; (3) the Law and good works; (4) the Gospel and justification; (5) the Holy Sacraments; (6) the nature and authority of the church; and (7) temporal authority.

[24] *Confession*, B2v.

[25] *Confession*, B2v: "We wish here to set out where there has been deviation from this clear, comprehensible, obvious, understanding of Christian teaching and confession of belief; deviation by Papists, Interimists, and *adiaphorists*, likewise Anabaptists, sacramentarians, and other misguided spirits."

[26] *Confession*, C4v: "To preserve this discipline . . . for use by father and mother He has prescribed the rod of correction; and by the authorities the use of the sword."

[27] See *Confession*, D2r: "the Anabaptists (die Widerteuffer) partly suspend the Law, in order to forbid Christians to have authorities, courts of Law, goods privately owned, and other things . . ."

[28] *Confession*, E1v: "Accordingly, God makes a man free from sins and death, justifies him and gives him new life, not on account of his works or worth . . . but entirely for the sake of Christ on whom alone he depends, enfolding the whole man in His innocence and righteousness."

[29] *Confession*, E2v.

[30] See Luther, "Concerning the Spirit and the Letter" in *Answer to the Hyperchristian, Hyperspiritual, and Hyperlearned Book by Goat Emser in Leipzig—Including Some Thoughts Regarding His Companion, The Fool Murner* (1521), LW 39:173–205.

[31] *Confession*, E2v.

[32] *Confession*, E2v-E3r: "In order that [the papists] may however leave Christ with something to do, so that he is not completely idle and so that he did not come to earth entirely to no purpose, they teach that Christ obtained grace for us by his efforts in having the real sin of our first parents no longer held against us, and in having faith, hope, and love inspired into us by God and thus preparing us henceforth to be able to earn forgiveness of sins, righteousness, life and blessing, through our good works."

[33] *Confession*, E3v-E4r.

[34] *Confession*, E3v: "Now even 'infused' righteousness, faith, hope and love, which, as they say Christ earned for us, and which he gives us through the Holy Spirit, can not free us from sins and make us righteous and blessed until and unless we use and exercise of them is our own work, then accordingly the immediate powerful consequence follows—so the argument would run—that we ourselves have also something to boast about in the sight of God, and *we can contribute something* to our justification and towards our bliss; apparently almost more, as it were than Christ the Lord, and indeed that we really become righteous and blessed *through the works of the Law and not through Christ at all*" (*emphasis added*).

[35] *Confession*, F4r.

[36] *Confession*, F4v.

[37] The key phrase for the Magdeburg pastors was δώσω σοι τὰς κλεῖδας τῆς βασιλείας τῶν οὐρανῶν.

[38] *Confession*, G1v.

[39] *Confession*, G2r-G2v: "Since [the papists] wish to set up the primacy of the Pope, confirming that he is the supreme head of the church, they have made abominable errors: first, that they say he is, by virtue of Divine ordinance and command of God a common bishop over all the churches. Secondly, by virtue of the same ordinance and command, that he alone has the power of the keys, and may distribute to others as and how he will. *Thirdly, that they assign to him both swords, and perfect power to govern both estates—spiritual and temporal*" (emphasis added).

[40] *Confession*, G3r: "Although it is not [God's] will that these spheres [civil and ecclesial authority] should be mixed up with one another, nevertheless, he ordained that one should serve the other, and should agree both in theory and practice, and should agree that each in his proper station in life according to his ability and judgment should promote the proper understanding and honor of God, and promote and advance the eternal bliss of all men committed to his care. Or if they cannot attain this, that they should at least see that people live peaceably and honorably in this civic community."

[41] *Confession*, G3v.

[42] *Confession*, G4r: "Temporal and household government are genuine ordinances of God . . . so that, accordingly, the work of regulating a household and temporal authority as long as they do not go against reason and the Word of God will please God."

[43] *Confession*, G4v.

[44] *Confession*, G4v.

[45] *Confession*, G4v: "Finally, we hope thus to eliminate any suspicion that we had initiated any innovations or had intended or wanted to do so, or had broken away from previous teaching of pure doctrine and pure worship of God which we have likewise not done. We want to make it quite clear that we are not now doing anything different, though we are now excommunicated and damned with a curse and threats of purgatory and condemned not only by our foes but even by our own brethren."

[46] *Confession*, H1r: "Other readers outside (this city) can find everything better and more fully expressed in Dr. Martin Luther's writings."

[47] "The Instruction of Justified Resistance" is equal in length to the first section, the "Confession" (43.5 pages compared to 44 pages). The "Instruction" is composed of five subsections, though these are not separated as chapters, *per se*. The "Instruction" begins with a somewhat lengthy introduction followed by an explication of the pastors' three central arguments for justified resistance, which is followed by a brief conclusion.

[48] *Confession*, M2v-M3r: "The other arguments, of which several are grounded in the written imperial laws, need not be repeated here since they are well known from the writings of several of the most distinguished present-day theologians with whom we, as too they with us, have had dealings in this business of justified resistance." See also the discussion of the *Torgau Declaration* pp. 50–51 and in WATr 3:631, no. 3810; 4:235, no, 4342; and 4:271, no. 4380 (1538–39). In all three *Table Talks*, Luther returned repeatedly to the constitutional argument that the emperor

is not a monarch ruling alone, he rules together with the Electors. Luther wrote: "These times are not the times of the martyrs, when Diocletian reigned alone and tyrannized Christians. This is a different empire, the emperor rules together with the seven electors. Without the seven the emperor has no authority . . . this empire is no longer a monarchy, where one alone rules (as with the Turks). If this was like Diocletian's empire, then we would have to readily submit to him and suffer" (WATr 4:273, no. 4380).

[49] *Confession*, H2r: "Darzu konnen Mitteldinge nicht mehr Mitteldinge heissen, wenn die Leute darzu gezwungen werden Sondern Sind Sünde verleugung unnd abfall von Gott."

[50] *Confession*, H2r-H2v. Here the pastors make an allusion to Melanchthon and his role in the *Torgau Declaration*.

[51] *Confession*, H2v: "All of [the Papists] know, however, or ought to know that in accordance with divine Law, natural Law, and secular Law, we cannot be condemned or attacked only on the basis of hearsay evidence without our case being heard."

[52] *Confession*, H3r: "They intend to stamp out our religion sooner than admit their injustice."

[53] *Confession*, H2v.

[54] *Confession*, H4v: "We are no political threat and only entreat that we may be given protection and that the preaching of Christ might be unforbidden."

[55] *Confession*, J1r.

[56] *Confession*, J1r, and Martin Luther, *Invocavit Sermons*, LW 51:77: "Had they heeded my admonition, I would have won them; if not, I would nevertheless not have torn them from it by the hair or employed any force, but simply allowed the Word to act and prayed for them."

[57] *Confession*, J1v: "We beseech your Imperial Majesty however, to graciously consider how grievous and unbearable it would be to your Imperial Majesty who is also God-fearing and wishes to be a Christian if he were to attack and persecute Christians and true members of Christ for the very reason that they elevate Christ and his Word too high and consider them too great and holy, and reflect how badly it would serve your Imperial Majesty on the Day of Judgment before the severe Court of Christ when you have to give reckoning of all your works and receive the merited reward."

[58] *Confession*, J3r, *emphasis in the original*.

[59] *Confession*, J3r.

[60] See *Confession*, J3r.

[61] See Martin Luther, *Treatise on Good Works*, LW 44:92: "[T]he power of the temporal authority, whether it does right or wrong, cannot harm the soul, but only our property—unless, of course, it should try openly to compel us to do wrong against God or men, as it did in the early church when the rulers were not yet Christian. . ."

[62] *Confession*, J3r: "Accordingly we beg and beseech most gracious Lord Emperor, your Imperial Majesty, for the sake of the bitter suffering, death and resurrection of our Lord Jesus Christ . . . and for the sake of the just and severe Judgment of God, that your Imperial Majesty should lift the Imperial Ban from us of Magdeburg and all innocent Christians."

[63] *Confession*, J3v: "And if we, like others who have begged your Imperial Majesty on our behalf in vain, if we cannot obtain this then we will bear witness against your Imperial Majesty on the Day of Judgment before Christ the Judge and will have to be accusers."

[64] *Confession*, J3v: "Your Imperial Majesty will also be to blame for forcing many pious and peace-loving Christians to take a stand in unavoidable resistance against your Imperial Majesty's pitiless, illegal, and unjust persecution."

[65] *Confession*, J3v.

[66] See 1 Macc 2:1–48.

[67] *Confession*, J4r-J4v: "This is similar to what Antiochus did in the time of the Maccabeans when he wanted to exterminate the church and God's people without effort."

[68] *Confession*, J4v-K1r.

[69] *Confession*, M3v: "But as in the whole German land there is now hardly any more than a little seed remaining of the pure untainted doctrine . . . thereby we are under the greatest compulsion to propagate right divine truth about justified resistance in these dire straits among people everywhere as much as we can, and thus regulate somewhat this despising suppression of Christ's word and his Church."

[70] *Confession*, K1v. This quotation lacks the vehemence of the cover-page quotation, but the import is still the same. The government must protect the law-abiding and punish the wicked.

[71] *Confession*, K2r: "this magistracy still remains accountable to God for the execution of its office with regard to its subjects, that is, it must maintain good, punish evil in everyone who deserves it, even in a superior. Paul excludes no one, nay, he makes a superior who becomes a tyrant an ordinance of the Devil." See also WATr 4:239, no. 4342 (February 7, 1539): "The emperor is not a monarch, who alone rules the German Empire (as the kings of England and France are); instead he rules together with the electors. Each of them is charged to take care of the empire. Each of them has a duty to encourage the good and resist that which would injure or prejudice the empire."

[72] *Confession*, K2v.

[73] See Martin Luther, *Temporal Authority*, LW 45.

[74] This position represents a concrete manifestation of Flacius's slogan, "*In casu confessionis et scandali nihil est adiaphora.*" It also reflects the position of the *Augsburg Confession* XVI: "Therefore, Christians are necessarily bound to obey their own magistrates and laws save only when commanded to sin; for then they ought to obey God rather than men. Acts 5, 29."

[75] *Confession*, K3r.

[76] *Confession*, K3v.

[77] See WATr 3:632, no. 3810: "But, if the emperor does make war upon us, and intends to destroy our preaching and our religion, or invade and destroy public life and economy (i.e., temporal and domestic government), then he is a tyrant. Therefore it is foolish to ask whether we may fight for upright, pure doctrine and religion. Of course we must fight for wife, children, servants and subjects; we are bound to defend them against wicked power. If I live, I will write an admonition for all states in the entire world, about armed defense; and demonstrate that all are bound to defend themselves and theirs against wicked power."

[78] *Confession*, K4v: "Our superiors want to eliminate with force in us and our successors this true insight and knowledge of God without which God cannot be honored and no man can be saved." See also Martin Luther, *Disputation Concerning the Right to Resist the Emperor* (May 8–9, 1539), WA 39 II:60:

> If one may resist the pope, one may also resist all the emperors and dukes who contrive to defend the pope . . . The pope . . . wishes . . . every soul . . . to go to hell for his sake. Hence it is necessary that one march against his soldiers that war under him and go out to meet them even though it mean a revolution. For we can not allow the damnation of souls. I am obliged to lay down my life for the emperor, but not my soul.

> If the emperor defends the pope, who is a wolf, one is not to yield or stand for it, but one must attack him . . . Self-defense is the natural course.

> The princes must resist the tyrants, a thing which the First Table also requires. The emperor and Ferdinand are seeking first and foremost to get our goods, but still under the cover of the pope." (The English translation of the *Disputation* appears in Lowell C. Green, "Resistance to Authority and Luther," *LQ* 6 [1954]: 346.)

[79] *Confession*, L1r.

[80] See n. 59 above.

[81] *Confession* L1r: "Christus Matth. 22 bestätigt es durch ein starken, ja, und setzet es beides zusammen dan man dem Keyser soll geben was des Keysers ist und daneben auch Gottes was Gottes ist" ("Give therefore to the emperor the things that are the emperor's, and to God the things that are God's").

[82] *Confession*, L1v. Interestingly, Luther makes nearly the same point; however, he uses Acts 5:29 ("We must obey God rather than any human authority.") to support his position. Luther writes: "Dear Lord, I am bound to obey you with body and good; command me according to your earthly power, and I will follow your command. But if you try to take from me my faith and Christian books, I will not obey" (WA 11:267. Quoted in Green, "Resistance to Authority and Luther," 342).

[83] The use of the family as the central metaphor for speaking of obedience was not accidental on the part of the pastors. The belief that the family represented the primary form of authority (*hierarchia oeconomia*) was strongly advanced by Luther. For example, in his exegesis of the Fourth Commandment in his *Large Catechism*, he writes: "In this commandment belongs a further statement regarding all kinds of obedience to persons in authority who have to command and to govern. For all authority flows and is propagated from the authority of parents."

[84] *Confession*, L2r.

[85] *Confession*, M1r.

[86] Generally considered one of the great "Christian" emperors, Theodosius I (c. 346–395) presided over the Ecumenical Council of 381. In 390, though, he was responsible for the massacre of nearly 7,000 people in Thessalonica. For that act, Ambrose excommunicated him. Theodosius repented and underwent eight months of strict penance.

[87] *Confession*, M4v. See also WATr 4:242, no. 4342 (February 7, 1539): "The emperor is not an absolute monarch, who governs alone at his whim. The electors have equal power and administration. He does not have the right to alone make laws and ordinances, much less does he have the right, power, or authority to wield the sword in order to vanquish the subjects and citizens of the empire, without the

sanction of law or the knowledge and consent of the whole empire. Therefore, Emperor Otto was wise when he ordained seven electors who together with the emperor would rule the empire. Had he not done that, it would not have stood and endured so long."

[88] *Confession* N3r: "As Christ himself bears witness (Matthew 25 [40]), whosoever you do to the least of my people you have done unto me."

[89] See Olson, "Theology of Revolution," 72: "In a city founded around the St. Moritz monastery, engaged in a struggle against an archbishop exiled from the Moritzburg, a Saxon duke named Moritz and an emperor who wore St. Moritz's sword, the Magdeburg theologians were pleased to make use of [this] theme."

[90] *Confession*, O3v.

[91] *Confession*, O4r.

[92] *Confession*, O4v.

[93] *Confession*, P2v.

[94] In making the point that they are brethren, the pastors also noted that they are fellow Germans being forced into submission by a "foreign yoke." They implied that though Charles is the rightful emperor, he is still not a German. So for the sake not only of the Gospel, but for Germany, lesser magistrates must come to their aid (*Confession*, P3v).

[95] *Confession*, Q2r: "Since therefore we must all sooner or later leave behind all that is temporal, how can we be better or more glorious evermore than as God wants to have it, namely, that we leave it all behind here for His sake . . . God will recompense us in the Eternal Life with great glory and eminence for what we risk and lose here for His sake."

[96] Matt 16:18.

[97] Ps 44:22.

[98] Luke 21:33.

[99] In fact, the city's official Web site (www.magdeburg.de) claims that Maurice had to give up the siege despite having vast numerical superiority.

[100] See Olson, "Theology of Revolution," 76: " 'Ja' said the duke, 'vertragen soll auch vertragen sein und bleiben.' "

CHAPTER 5: CONCLUSION

[1] For a dramatic example of this, see Brad S. Gregory, *Salvation at Stake: Christian Martyrdom in Early Modern Europe* (Cambridge: Harvard University Press, 1999).

[2] Theodore Beza, *De Haereticis a ciuili Magistratu puniendis Libellus, aduersus Martini Bellii farraginewm, & nouorum Academicorum sectam, Theodoro Beza Vezelio aucture* (Geneva: Olivia Roberti Stephani, 1554), 113.

[3] Martin Bucer (1491–1551) was the leader of the Reformation in Strassbourg, France.

[4] Theodore Beza, *Du droit des magistrats sur leurs subiets. Traitte tres-necessaire en ce temps, pour aduertir de leur deuoir, tant les Magistrats que les Subiets: publie par ceux de Magdebourg l'an M D L: & maintenant reueu & augmente de plusieurs raisons & exemples* (n. p., 1574), question 3.

[5] It is interesting to note that even in 1553 in his *Godly Letter of Warning or Admonition to the Faithful in London, Newcastle, and Berwick*, Knox advocates only passive resistance: "Flee from that abominable idol, the maintainers whereof shall not escape the vengeance of God. Let it be known to your posterity that you were Christians and not idolaters; that you learned Christ in time of rest, and boldly professed him in time of trouble. . . . For avoiding of idolatry you may perchance be compelled to leave your native country and realm; but obeyers of idolatry, without end, shall be compelled, body and soul, to burn in hell. . . . For avoiding of idolatry you may fall in the hands of earthly tyrants; but obeyers, maintainers, and consenters to idolatry shall not escape the hands of the living God. For avoiding idolatry, your children shall be deprived of father, of friends, riches, and of earthly rest; but by obeying idolatry they shall be left without the knowledge of his word, and without hope of his kingdom" (http://www.swrb.com/newslett/actualnls/GodlyLtr.htm).

[6] John Knox, *The Works of John Knox* (6 vols.; ed. David Laing; Edinburgh: Bannatyne Club, 1845–64), II:453–54.

[7] Quentin Skinner notes the transition began in Magdeburg but dismisses it. He argues that the *Confession* deals with the issue of Romans "scantly." (See Quentin Skinner, *The Reformation* [vol. 2 of *The Foundations of Modern Political Thought*; Cambridge: Cambridge University Pess, 1978], II:227, n. 1.) I disagree; the reinterpretation of Rom 13:1 is, in fact, an important aspect of the *Confession*'s argument.

[8] John Knox, *The Appellation from the Sentence Pronounced by the Bishops and Clergy: Addressed to the Nobility and Estates of Scotland* (1558) (http://www.swrb.com/newslett/ actualnls/Appellat.htm)

[9] See David M. Whitford, "John Adams, John Ponet, and a Lutheran Influence on the American Revolution," *LQ* XV.2 (2001): 143–58.

[10] Johann Sleiden, *The State of Religion and the Commonwealth during the Reign of Emperor Charles the Fifth* (trans. John Daus; London, 1560): "In the month of April, the ministers of the church set forth in writing, wherein they recite the confession of their doctrine, and declare how it is lawful for the inferior magistrate to defend himself against the superior, compelling him to forsake the truth."

[11] Hans Christoph von Hase, *Die Gestalt der Kirche Luthers: Der Casus Confessionis im Kampf des Matthias Flacius gegen das Interim von 1548* (Göttingen: Vandenhoeck & Ruprecht, 1940), 4. Quoted in Uwe Siemon-Netto, *The Fabricated Luther* (St. Louis: Concordia, 1995), 91f.

[12] For a classic discussion on this aspect of politics, see Harold Lasswell, *Politics: Who Gets What, When, How* (New York: Meridian Books, 1958).

[13] For a discussion on this dynamic, see Charles Tilly, "Reflections on the History of European State-Making," in *The Formation of National States in Western Europe* (ed. Charles Tilly; Princeton: Princeton University Press, 1975), 3–83; and Joseph R. Strayer, *On the Medieval Origins of the Modern State* (Princeton: Princeton University Press, 1970).

[14] Martin Luther, "Ordinance of a Common Chest," LW 45:172.

BIBLIOGRAPHY

Akers, Charles W. "Calvinism and the American Revolution." In *The Heritage of John Calvin: Heritage Hall Lectures, 1960–1970*. Edited by John H. Bratt. Grand Rapids: Eerdmans, 1972.

Allen, J. W. *A History of Political Thought in the Sixteenth Century*. London: Methuen Press, 1957.

Althaus, Paul. *The Ethics of Martin Luther*. Translated by Robert C. Schultz. Philadelphia: Fortress, 1972.

———. *Der Geist der lutherischen Ethik im Augsburgerishen Bekenntnis*. Munich: Christian Kaiser, 1930.

———. "Luthers Lehre von den beiden Reichen im Feuer der Kritik." *Lutherjahrbuch* 24 (1957): 40–67.

Anderson, William K. "Luther and Calvin: A Contrast in Politics." *Religious Life* 9 (Spring 1940): 256–67.

Anselm, Archbishop of Canterbury. *Cur Deus Homo: Why God became Man, and The Virgin Conception and Original Sin*. Translated, introduction, and notes by Joseph M. Colleran. Albany: Magi Books, c. 1969.

Aquinas, Thomas. *Summa Theologia*. Translated and comments by T. C. O'Brien O. P. New York: Black Friars in conjunction with McGraw Hill, 1965.

Aristotle. *Nichomachean Ethics*. Translated by Martin Ostwald. Indianapolis: Bobbs-Merrill, 1962.

———. *Politics*. Translated by Carnes Lord. Chicago: University of Chicago Press, 1984.

Augustine, St. Aurelius. *The Basic Writings of Saint Augustine*. Edited, introduction, and notes by Whitney J. Oates. 2 vols. Grand Rapids: Baker Books, 1992. Originally published by Random House, 1948.

Bagchi, David. *Luther's Earliest Opponents: Catholic Controversialists, 1518–1525*. Minneapolis: Fortress, 1991.

Bainton, Roland H. *Here I Stand: A Life of Martin Luther*. New York: Abingdon-Cokesbury, 1950.

————. *The Reformation of the Sixteenth Century*. Boston: Beacon Press, 1952. Enlarged edition with foreword by Jaroslav Pelikan, 1985.

Barth, Karl. *Community, State, and Church: Three Essays*. Introduction by Will Herberg. Garden City: Doubleday, 1960.

————. *Eine Schweiser Stimme 1938–1945*. Zollikon-Zürich: Evangelischer Verlag, 1945.

Bast, Robert J. "From Two Kingdoms to Two Tables: The Ten Commandments and the Christian Magistrate." *Archiv für Reformationsgeschichte* 89 (1998): 79–95.

Bayer, Oswald. "Barmen zwischen Barth und Luther." In *Luther und Barth = Veröffentlichungen der Luther-Akademie Ratenburg*. Band 13. Edited by Joachim Heubach. Erlangen: Martin Luther-Verlag, 1988.

Baylor, Michael. "Introduction to Lutheran Resistance Theory and the Imperial Constitution." *Lutheran Quarterly* 2 (1988): 185–207.

————. "Lutheran Contributions to Sixteenth Century Resistance Theory." Paper presented to the American Historical Association. Boston, Mass., December 30, 1970.

————. "Theology and Politics in the Thought of Thomas Müntzer: The Case of the Elect." *Archiv für Reformationsgeschichte* 79 (1988): 81–101.

————. "Thomas Müntzer's First Publication." *Sixteenth Century Journal* 17.4 (1986): 451–59.

————. "Thomas Müntzer's *Prague Manifesto*." *Mennonite Quarterly Review* (1988): 30–57.

Bekentnis Unterricht und Vermanung der Pfarrherrn und Prediger der Christlichen Kirchen zu Magdeburgk (1550). Reprinted in Friedrich Hortleder, *Handlungen und Ausschreiben . . . von Rechtmässigkeit des Teutschen Kriegs Karls des Fünfften*. Gotha, 1615.

Beker, Johann Christiaan. *The Triumph of God: The Essence of Paul's Thought*. Translated by Loren T. Stuckenbruck. Minneapolis: Fortress, 1990.

Benert, Richard Roy. "Inferior Magistrates in Sixteenth-Century Political and Legal Thought." Ph.D. diss., University of Minnesota, 1967.

Benzing, Josef. *Lutherbibliographie: Verzeichnis der Gedruckten Schriften Martin Luthers bis zu dessen Tod*. Baden-Baden: Heitz, 1966.

Berger, Peter. *The Sacred Canopy: Elements of a Sociological Theory of Religion*. Garden City: Doubleday Anchor, 1969.

Beza, Theodore. *Du droit des magistrats sur leurs subiets. Traitte tres-necessaire en ce temps, pour aduertir de leur deuoir, tant les Magistrats que les Subiets: publie par ceux de Magdebourg l'an M D L: & maintenant reueu*

& augmente de plusieurs raisons & exemples. n. p., 1574.

———. De Haereticis a ciuili Magistratu puniendis Libellus, aduersus Martini Bellii farraginewm, & nouorum Academicorum sectam, Theodoro Beza Vezelio aucture. Geneva: Olivia Roberti Stephani, 1554.

Blickle, Peter. Communal Reformation: The Quest for Salvation in Sixteenth-Century Germany. Atlantic Highlands: Humanities Press, 1992.

———. Die Reformation im Reich. Stuttgart: Ulmer, 1982.

———. The Revolution of 1525: The German Peasants' War from a new Perspective. Baltimore: Johns Hopkins University Press, 1981.

Bornkamm, Heinrich. "Die theologischen Thesen Luthers bei der Heidelberger Disputation 1518 und seine theologia Crucis." In Luther, Gestalt und Wirkungen: Schriften des Vereins für Reformationsgeschichte. Vol. 5, no. 81. Gütersloh: Gütersloher Verlagshaus Gerd Mohn, 1975.

Bonhoeffer, Dietrich. Ethics. Edited by Eberhard Bethge. Translated by Neville Horton Smith. New York: Macmillian, 1955. Paperback edition, 1965.

Bossy, John. Christianity in the West, 1400–1700. Oxford: Oxford University Press, 1985.

Bouwsma, William J. John Calvin: A Sixteenth Century Portrait. Oxford: Oxford University Press, 1988.

Bowle, John. Western Political Thought: An Historical Introduction from the Origins to Rousseau. New York: Oxford University Press, 1949.

Brady, Thomas A. Protestant Politics: Jacob Sturm (1489–1553) and the German Reformation. Atlantic Highlands: Humanities Press, 1995.

Brandt, Dwaine Charles. "The City of Magdeburg Before and After the Reformation." Ph.D. diss., University of Washington, 1975.

Braaten, Carl E. "Protestants and Natural Law." First Things 19 (January 1992): 20–26.

Brecht, Martin. "Divine Right and Human Rights in Luther." In Martin Luther and the Modern Mind: Freedom, Conscience, Toleration, and Rights. Edited by Manfred Hoffman. Vol. 22 of Toronto Studies in Theology. New York: Edwin Mellen Press, 1985.

———. Martin Luther I: His Road to Reformation, 1483–1521. Translated by James L. Schaaf. Philadelphia: Fortress, 1985.

———. Martin Luther II: Shaping and Defining the Reformation, 1521–1532. Translated by James L. Schaaf. Philadelphia: Fortress, 1990.

———. Martin Luther III: The Preservation of the Church, 1532–1546. Translated by James L. Schaaf. Philadelphia: Fortress, 1993.

Bubenheimer, Ulrich. *Thomas Müntzer: Herkunft und Bildung*. Leiden: E. J. Brill, 1989.

Buck, Lawrence, and Jonathan Zophy, eds. *The Social History of the Reformation*. Columbus: Ohio State University Press, 1972.

Calvin, John. *Institutes of the Christian Religion*. Vols. 20–21 of *The Library of Christian Classics*. Edited by John Baillie et al. Translated by Ford Lewis Battles. Philadelphia: Westminster Press, 1960.

———. *John Calvin on God and Political Duty*. 2d ed. Edited by John T. McNeill. Indianapolis: Westminster Press, 1956.

Cameron, Euan. *The European Reformation*. Oxford: Clarendon Press, 1991.

Cantor, Norman F. *Inventing the Middle Ages: The Lives, Works, and Ideas of the Great Medievalists of the Twentieth Century*. New York: William Morrow, 1991.

Cargill Thompson, W. D. J. "Luther and the Right of Resistance to the Emperor." In *Church, Society, and Politics*. Edited Derek Baker. Oxford: Basil Blackwell for The Ecclesiastical History Society, 1975.

———. *The Political Thought of Martin Luther*. Edited by Philip Broadhead. Totowa: Barnes & Noble Books, 1984.

Carlyle, R. W., and A. J. Carlyle. *A History of Medieval Political Theory in the West*. New York: Barnes & Noble, 1964.

Collange, Jean François. "Droit á la résistance et réformation." *Revue d'Historie et de Philosophie Réligieuses* 65 (1985): 245–55.

Cooper, John W. "The Outlines of Political Theology in the Protestant Reformation." In *Studies on Religion and Politics*. Edited by James V. Schall and Jerome J. Hanus. Lanham: University Press of America, 1986.

Davies, Rupert Eric. *The Problem of Authority in the Continental Reformers: A Study in Luther, Zwingli, and Calvin*. London: The Epworth Press, 1946.

Dickens, A. G. *The German Nation and Martin Luther*. New York: Harper & Row, 1974.

———, and John Tonkin, with Kenneth Powell. *The Reformation in Historical Thought*. Cambridge: Harvard University Press, 1985.

Dowey, Edward A. "Law in Luther and Calvin." *Theology Today* 41 (July 1984): 146–53.

Duchrow, Ulrich, and Wolfgang Huber, eds. *Die Ambivalenz der Zweireicheslehre in lutherischen Kirchen des 20. Jahrhunderts*. Gütersloh: Gütersloher Verlagshaus, 1976.

DuPlessis, L. M. "Calvin on State and Politics according to the

Institutes." In *John Calvin's Institutes.* Edited by B. Van der Walt et al. Potchefstroom, South Africa: Institute for Reformation Studies, 1986.

Durkheim, Emile. *The Elementary Forms of Religious Life.* New York: Free Press, 1965.

Ebeling, Gerhard. *Luther: An Introduction to His Thought.* Philadelphia: Fortress, 1970.

Edwards, Mark U., Jr. *Luther and the False Brethren.* Stanford: Stanford University Press, 1975.

———. *Luther's Last Battles: Politics and Polemics, 1531–1546.* Ithaca: Cornell University Press, 1983.

———. *Printing, Propaganda, and Martin Luther.* Berkeley: University of California Press, 1994.

Erasmus, Desiderius. *Annotations on Romans.* In vol. 56 of *Collected Works of Erasmus.* Edited by Robert D. Sider. Translated and annotated by John B. Payne, Albert Rabil Jr., Robert D. Sider, and Warren S. Smith Jr. Toronto: University of Toronto Press, 1994.

Estes, James M., ed. *Whether secular government has the right to wield the sword in matters of faith: a controversy in Nürnberg in 1530 over freedom of worship and authority of secular government in spiritual matters: five documents translated, with an introduction and notes.* Toronto: Centre for Reformation and Renaissance Studies, 1994.

Fabian, Ekkehart. *Die Entstehung des Schmalkaldischen Bundes und seiner Verfassung, 1524/29–1531/35; Bruck, Philipp von Hessen und Jakob Sturm. Darstellung und Quellen mit einer Brück-Bibliographie.* Tübingen: Osiandersche Buchhandlung, Kommissionsverlag, 1962.

Figgis, John Neville. *Studies of Political Thought from Gerson to Grotius, 1414–1625.* Cambridge: The University Press, 1956.

Fowler, James W. *Stages of Faith.* San Francisco: Harper & Row, 1981.

Forde, Gerhard O. *On Being a Theologian of the Cross: Reflections on Luther's Heidelberg Disputation, 1518.* Grand Rapids: Eerdmans, 1997.

———. *The Law-Gospel Debate: An Interpretation of its Historical Development.* Minneapolis: Augsburg, 1969.

———. "Law and Gospel in Luther's Hermeneutic." *Interpretation* 37 (1983): 240–52.

———. *Theology Is for Proclamation.* Minneapolis: Fortress, 1990.

Franz, Günther. *Quellen zur Geschichte des Bauernkrieges.* Darmstadt: Oldenbourg, 1963.

Frei, Hans W. *Types of Christian Theology.* New Haven: Yale University Press, 1992.

Friesen, Abraham. *Reformation and Utopia: The Marxist Interpretation of the Reformation and its Antecedents.* Wiesbaden: F. Steiner, 1974.

———. *Thomas Muentzer, a Destroyer of the Godless: The Making of a Sixteenth-Century Religious Revolutionary.* Berkeley: University of California Press, 1990.

Gamble, Richard C. "The Christian and the Tyrant: Beza and Knox on Political Resistance Theory." *Westminster Theological Journal* 46 (1984): 125–39.

Geertz, Clifford. *The Interpretation of Cultures.* New York: Basic Books, Harper Collins, 1973.

George, Timothy. *Theology of the Reformers.* Nashville: Broadman, 1988.

Gerrish, Brian A. *Grace and Reason.* Oxford: Oxford University Press, 1962.

———. "Strasbourg Revisited: The Augsburg Confession in a Reformed Perspective." In *The Augsburg Confession in Ecumenical Perspective: With Anglican, Baptist, Methodist, Orthodox, Reformed, and Roman Catholic Contributions.* Edited by Harding Meyer. Stuttgart: Kreuz Verlag, Breitshol Gmbh. for the Lutheran World Federation, 1980.

Goertz, Hans-Jürgen, ed. *Profiles of the Radical Reformers.* Scottdale, Penn.: Herald Press, 1982.

Goldhagen, Daniel Jonah. *Hitler's Willing Executioners: Ordinary Germans and the Holocaust.* New York: Alfred Knopf, 1996.

Gregory, Brad S. *Salvation at Stake: Christian Martyrdom in Early Modern Europe.* Cambridge: Harvard University Press, 1999.

Gritsch, Eric W. *Martin—God's Court Jester: Luther in Retrospect.* Philadelphia: Fortress, 1983.

———. *Reformer without a Church: The Life and Thought of Thomas Muentzer 1488?–1525.* Philadelphia: Fortress, 1967.

———. "The Use and Abuse of Luther's Political Advice." *Lutherjahrbuch* 57 (1990): 207–19.

———. *Thomas Muentzer: A Tragedy of Errors.* Minneapolis: Fortress, 1989.

Hagan, Kenneth. "The Testament of a Worm: Luther on Testament to 1525." *Consensus* 8.1 (1982): 14–22.

Hamilton, Alexander. *The Federalist Papers: A Collection of Essays Written in Support of the Constitution of the United States: from the Original Text of Alexander Hamilton, James Madison, John Jay.* Selected and edited by Roy P. Fairfield. Baltimore: Johns Hopkins University Press, 1981.

Härle, Wilfred. "Die politische Verantwortung der Kirche—aus evangelischer Sicht." Pages 141–51 in *Glaube—Bekenntnis—Kirchenrecht*. Hannover: Lutherisches Verlagshaus, 1989.

Harran, Marilyn J. "Luther and Freedom of Thought." In *Martin Luther and the Modern Mind: Freedom, Conscience, Toleration, and Rights*. Edited by Manfred Hoffman. Vol. 22 of Toronto Studies in Theology. New York: Edwin Mellen Press, 1985.

Headley, John F. "The Reformation as a Crisis in the Understanding of Tradition." *Archiv für Reformationsgeschichte* 78 (1987): 5–22.

Hildebrandt, Ester. "The Magdeburg *Bekentnis* as a Possible Link between German and English Resistance Theories in the Sixteenth Century." *Archiv für Reformationsgeschichte* 73(1982): 227–53.

Hillerbrand, Hans. *The Reformation*. Grand Rapids: Baker, 1993.

Höpfl, Harro. *The Christian Polity of John Calvin*. Cambridge: Cambridge University Press, 1982.

———, ed. and trans. *Luther and Calvin on Secular Authority*. Cambridge: Cambridge University Press, 1992.

Hoffman, Friedrich Wilhelm. *Geschichte der Stadt Magdeburg, nach den Quellen bearbeitet*. 2 vols. Magdeburg: A. Rathke, 1847.

Hoffmann, Manfred, ed. *Martin Luther and the Modern Mind: Freedom, Conscience, Toleration, and Rights*. Vol. 22 of Toronto Studies in Theology. New York: Edwin Mellen Press, 1985.

———. "Reformation and Toleration." In *Martin Luther and the Modern Mind: Freedom, Conscience, Toleration, and Rights*. Edited by Manfred Hoffman. Vol. 22 of Toronto Studies in Theology. New York: Edwin Mellen Press, 1985.

Holl, Karl. *The Cultural Significance of the Reformation*. Translated by Karl and Barbara Hertz and John H. Lichtblau. New York: Meridian, 1959.

Iserloh, Erwin. "The Imperial Diet of Augsburg." In *Reformation and Counter Reformation*. Vol. 10 of *The History of the Church*. Edited by Hubert Jedin and John Dolan. Translated by Anslem Briggs and Peter W. Becker. New York: The Seabury Press, 1975.

———, and Gerhard Müller, eds. *Luther und die politische Welt*. Vol. 9 of *Historische Forschungen*. Stuttgart: Franz Steiner, 1984.

Jenni, Ernst, and Claus Westermann. *Theological Lexicon of the Old Testament: Volume One*. Translated by Mark E. Biddle. Peabody: Hendrickson, 1997.

Keen, Ralph. *Divine and Human Authority in Reformation Thought: German Theologians on Political Order, 1520–1555*. Nieuwkoop, Netherlands: B. de Graaf, 1997.

Ketcham, Ralph, ed. *The Anti-Federalist Papers and The Constitutional Convention Debates*. New York: New American Library, 1986.

Kingdon, Robert M. "Calvinism and Democracy." In *The Heritage of John Calvin: Heritage Hall Lectures, 1960–1970*. Edited by John H. Bratt. Grand Rapids: Eerdmans. 1972.

———. *Church and Society in Reformation Europe*. London: Valiorum Reprints, 1985.

———. "The First Expression of Theodore Beza's Political Ideas." *Archiv für Reformationsgeschichte* 46 (1955): 88–100.

———, ed. *Transition and Revolution: Problems and Issues of European Renaissance and Reformation History*. Minneapolis: Burgess, 1974.

Klan, J. S. "Luther's Resistance Teaching and the German Church under Hitler." *Journal of Religious History* 14 (1987/88): 432–44.

Kolb, Robert. *Nicholas von Amsdorf (1483–1565): Popular Polemics in the Preservation of Luther's Legacy*. Nieuwkoop, Netherlands: B. de Graaf, 1978.

Kouri, E. I., and Tom Scott, eds. *Politics and Society in Reformation Europe: Essays for Sir Geoffrey Elton on His Sixty-Fifth Birthday*. London: MacMillian, 1987.

Lasswell, Harold. *Politics: Who Gets What, When, and How*. New York: Meridian, 1958.

Lau, Franz. *Luthers Lehre von den beiden Reichen*. Berlin: Evangelische Verlagsanstalt, 1952.

Lindbeck, George A. "Modernity and Luther's Understanding of the Freedom of the Christian." In *Martin Luther and the Modern Mind: Freedom, Conscience, Toleration, and Rights*. Edited by Manfred Hoffman. Vol. 22 of Toronto Studies in Theology. New York: Edwin Mellen Press, 1985.

———. *The Nature of Doctrine: Religion and Theology in a Post-Liberal Age*. Philadelphia: Westminster, 1984.

Lindberg, Carter. "Conflicting Models of Ministry: Luther, Karlstadt, and Müntzer." *Concordia Theological Quarterly* 41.4 (1977): 35–50.

———. *The European Reformations*. Oxford: Blackwell, 1996.

———. *Beyond Charity: Reformation Initiatives for the Poor*. Minneapolis: Fortress, 1993.

———. "Introduction." In *Peace and the Just War Tradition: Lutheran Perspectives in the Nuclear Age*. Edited by Michael J. Stelmachowicz. St. Louis: Concordia, 1986.

———. "Justification by Faith Alone: *The* Lutheran Proposal to the Churches." *New Conversations* 10.2 (1988): 31–41.

———. "Luther's Critique of the Ecumenical Assumption that Doctrine Divides but Service Unites." *Journal of Ecumenical Studies* 27 (1990): 679–96.

———. "Tainted Greatness: Luther's Attitudes toward Judaism and their Historical Reception." In *Tainted Greatness: Antisemitism and Cultural Heroes*. Edited by Nancy A. Harrowitz. Philadelphia: Temple University Press, 1994.

———. "Theology and Politics: Luther the Radical and Müntzer the Reactionary." *Encounter* 37.4 (1976): 356–71.

Loewenich, Walter von. *Luthers theologia crucis*. 5th ed. Wittenberg: Luther-Verlag, 1967.

———. *Luther's Theology of the Cross*. Translated by Herbert J. A. Bouman. Minneapolis: Augsburg, 1976.

Lohse, Bernhard. *Martin Luther: An Introduction to His Life and Work*. Translated by Robert C. Schultz. Philadelphia: Fortress, 1986.

———. *Martin Luther's Theology: Its Historical and Systematic Development*. Edited and translated by Roy A. Harrisville. Philadelphia: Augsburg, 1999.

Luther, Martin. *D. Martin Luthers Werke, Kritische Gesamtaugsgabe*. 100 vols. Weimar: Herman Böhlaus Nachfolger, 1883–.

———. *Luther's Works*. 55 vols. General editors Jaroslav Pelikan and Helmut T. Lehmann. St. Louis: Concordia, and Philadelphia: Muhlenberg and Fortress, 1955–80.

Machiavelli, Niccolò. *The Prince*. Translated by Harvey C. Mansfield Jr. Chicago: University of Chicago Press, 1985.

Mack, Phyllis, and Margaret C., eds. *Politics and Culture in Early Modern Europe: Essays in Honor of H. G. Koenigsberger Jacob*. New York: Cambridge University Press, 1987.

Madison, James et al. *The Federalist Papers*. Introduction by Clinton Rossiter. New York: Mentor, 1961.

Maltby, William S., ed. *Reformation Europe: A Guide to Research, Volume 2*. St. Louis: Center for Reformation Research, 1992.

Maurer, Wilhelm. *Die Kirche und ihr Recht: Gesammelte Aufsätze zum evangelishen Kirchenrecht*. Edited by Gerhard Müller and Gottfried Seebaß. Tubingen: Mohr, 1976.

McGrath, Alister E. *The Intellectual Origins of the European Reformation*. Oxford: Blackwell, 1987.

———. *Luther's Theology of the Cross*. Oxford: Basil Blackwell, 1985.

———. *Reformation Thought: An Introduction*. 2d ed. Cambridge: Blackwell, 1993.

Mitchell, Joshua. "The Equality of All under the One in Luther and Rosseau: Thoughts on Christianity and Political Theory." *Journal of Religion* 72 (1992): 351–65.

———. "Protestant Thought and Republican Spirit: How Luther Enchanted the World." *American Political Science Review*. 86.3 (September 1992): 688–95.

Moeller, Bernd. *Imperial Cities and the Reformation: Three Essays.* Edited and translated by H. C. Eric Midelfort and Mark U. Edwards Jr. Durham: Labyrinth, 1972. Reprinted in 1982.

Moltmann, Jürgen. "Reformation and Revolution." In *Martin Luther and the Modern Mind: Freedom, Conscience, Toleration, and Rights.* Edited by Manfred Hoffman. Vol. 22 of Toronto Studies in Theology. New York: Edwin Mellen Press, 1985.

Mouw, Richard J. *The God Who Commands.* Notre Dame: University of Notre Dame Press, 1990.

Mueller, William A. *Church and State in Luther and Calvin: A Comparative Study.* Nashville: Broadman, 1954.

Müller, Gerhard. "Martin Luther and the Political World of his Time," In *Politics and Society in Reformation Europe.* Edited by E. I. Kouri and Tom Scott. New York: St. Martin's, 1983.

———. *Reformation und Stadt: Zur Rezeption der evangelischen Verkündigung.* Abhandlungen der Geistes—und Sozialwissenschaftlichen Klasse, Akademie der Wissenschaften und der Literatur (Mainz), 1981/11. Wiesbaden: Franz Steiner, 1981.

Muller, Richard A. "Calvin, Beza, and the Exegetical History of Romans 13:1–7." In *Calvin and the State.* Edited by Peter De Klerk. Grand Rapids: Calvin Studies Society, 1993.

Müntzer, Thomas. *The Collected Works of Thomas Müntzer.* Edited and translated by Peter Matheson. Edinburgh: T & T Clark, 1988.

Nygren, Anders. *Agape and Eros.* Translated by Philip S. Watson. Philadelphia: Westminster, 1953.

Oberman, Heiko. *The Dawn of the Reformation: Essays in Late Medieval and Early Reformation Thought.* Edinburgh: T & T Clark, 1986.

———. *The Impact of the Reformation.* Grand Rapids: Eerdmans, 1994.

———. *Luther: Man between God and the Devil.* Translated by Eileen Walliser-Schwarzbart. New York: Image Books, Doubleday, 1982.

———. *The Reformation: Roots and Ramifications.* Translated by Andrew Colin Gow. Grand Rapids: Eerdmans, 1994.

Olson, Oliver K. "Matthias Flacius Illyricus." In *Shapers of Religious Traditions in Germany, Switzerland, and Poland, 1560–1600.* Edited by

Jill Raitt. New Haven: Yale University Press, 1981.

———. "Theology of Revolution: Magdeburg, 1550–1551." *Sixteenth Century Journal* 3.1 (April 1972): 66–79.

Ozment, Steven. *The Age of Reform: 1250–1550: An Intellectual and Religious History of Late Medieval and Reformation Europe.* New Haven: Yale University Press, 1980.

———. *Homo Spiritualis: A Comparative Study of the Anthropology of Johannes Tauler, Jean Gerson, and Martin Luther (1509–1516) in the Context of their Theological Thought.* Leiden: E. J. Brill, 1969.

———. "Luther's Political Legacy." In *German-American Interrelations: Heritage and Challenge.* Tübingen: Tübingen University Press, 1989.

———. *Protestants: The Birth of a Revolution.* New York: Doubleday, 1992.

———, ed. *Reformation Europe: A Guide to Research.* St. Louis: Center for Reformation Research, 1982.

Pelikan, Jaroslav. *The Christian Tradition: A History of the Development of Doctrine.* Vol. 4 of *Reformation of Church and Dogma (1300–1700).* Chicago: University of Chicago Press, 1984.

Pesch, Otto Hermann. "Free by Faith: Luther's Contribution to a Theological Anthropology." In *Martin Luther and the Modern Mind: Freedom, Conscience, Toleration, and Rights.* Edited by Manfred Hoffman. Vol. 22 of *Toronto Studies in Theology.* New York: Edwin Mellen Press, 1985.

Peterson, Luther D. "Justus Menius, Philipp Melanchthon, and the 1547 Treatise, *Von der Notwehr Unterrich.*" *Archiv für Reformationsgeschichte* 81 (1990): 138–57.

———. "Melanchthon on Resisting the Emperor: The *Von der Notwehr Unterricht* of 1546." In *Regnum, Religio, et Ratio: Essays Presented to Robert M. Kingdon.* Vol. 8 of *Sixteenth Century Essays and Studies.* Kirksville: Sixteenth Century Journal Publishers, 1987.

Ponet, John Bishop of Rochester and Worcester. *A Short Treatise of Politike Power, and of the true obedience which subjects owe to kings and other civil governors, with an exhortation to all true natural Englishmen.* Strassbourg, 1566.

Raitt, Jill, ed. *Christian Spirituality: High Middle Ages and Reformation.* New York: Crossroads, 1988.

Repgen, Konrad. "What Is a 'Religious War'?" In *Politics and Society in Reformation Europe: Essays for Sir Geoffrey Elton on his Sixty-Fifth Birthday.* Edited by E. I. Kouri and Tom Scott. London: MacMillian, 1987.

Rublack, Hans-Christoph. "Reformation and Society." In *Martin Luther and the Modern Mind: Freedom, Conscience, Toleration, and Rights.* Edited by Manfred Hoffman. Vol. 22 of Toronto Studies in Theology. New York: Edwin Mellen Press, 1985.

Rupp, Gordon. *Patterns of Reformation.* Philadelphia: Fortress, 1969.

Scheible, Heinz. *Das Widerstandsrecht als Problem der deutsche Protestanten 1523–1546.* Gütersloh: Gütersloher Verlagshaus Gerd Mohn, 1969.

Schilling, Heinz. "Veni Vidi Deus Vixit—Karl V. zwischen Religionskreig und Religionsfrieden." *Archiv für Reformationsgeschichte* 89 (1998): 144–66.

Schwarz, Hans. *True Faith in the True God: An Introduction to Luther's Life and Thought.* Translated by Mark William Worthing. Minneapolis: Augsburg, 1996.

Schulze, Winfried. "Zwingli, lutherisches Widerstandsdenken, monar-chomaschischer Widerstand." In *Zwingli und Europa.* Edited by P. Blickle, A. Lindt, and A. Schindler. Gütersloh: Gütersloher Verlagshaus Gerd Mohn, 1985.

Scott, Tom, and Bob Scribner, trans. and eds. *The German Peasants' War: A History in Documents.* Atlantic Highlands: Humanities Press, 1991.

Seebaß, Gottfried. "Die Augsburger Kirchenordnung von 1537 in ihrem historischen und theologischen Zussammenhang." In *Die Augsburger Kirchenordnung von 1537 und ihr Umfeld.* Edited by Reinhard Schwartz. Gütersloh: Mohn, 1988.

Shirer, William L. *The Rise and Fall of the Third Reich: A History of Nazi Germany.* New York: Simon & Schuster, 1960.

Shoenberger, Cynthia Grant. "The *Confession* of Magdeburg and the Lutheran Doctrine of Resistance." Ph.D. diss., Columbia University, 1972.

———. "The Development of the Lutheran Theory of Resistance: 1523–1530." *Sixteenth Century Journal* 8.1 (April 1977): 61–76.

———. "Luther and the Justifiability of Resistance to Legitimate Authority." *The Journal of the History of Ideas* 40 (1979): 3–20.

Siemon-Netto, Uwe. "The Luther Cliché: On Clichés, the *Zeitgeist,* and Modernity, a Refutation of the Stereotype that Luther's Doctrine of the Two Realms Fostered German Quietism under Hilter, Focusing on the Lutheran Roots of Carl Goerdeler's Resistance and the East German Revolution." Ph.D. diss., Boston University, 1992.

———. *The Fabricated Luther: The Rise and Fall of the Shirer Myth.* Foreword by Peter L. Berger. St. Louis: Concordia, 1995.

Skinner, Quentin. "The Origins of the Calvinist Theory of Revolution."

In *After the Reformation: Essays in Honor of J. H. Hexter.* Edited by Barbara C. Malament. Philadelphia: University of Pennsylvania Press, 1980.

———. *The Reformation.* Vol. 2 of *The Foundations of Modern Political Thought.* Cambridge: Cambridge University Press, 1978.

Smith, Jonathan Z. *Imagining Religion: From Babylon to Jonestown.* Chicago: University of Chicago Press, 1982.

Spitz, Lewis W. "The Christian in Church and State." In *Martin Luther and the Modern Mind: Freedom, Conscience, Toleration, and Rights.* Edited by Manfred Hoffman. Vol. 22 of Toronto Studies in Theology. New York: Edwin Mellen Press, 1985.

Stayer, James M. *The German Peasants' War and Anabaptist Community of Goods.* Montreal: McGill-Queen's University Press, 1991.

Stevenson, William R. *Sovereign Grace: The Place and Significance of Christian Freedom in John Calvin's Political Thought.* New York: Oxford University Press, 1999.

Strayer, Joseph R. *On the Medieval Origins of the Modern State.* Princeton: Princeton University Press, 1970.

Thompson, John L. "Patriarchs, Polygamy, and Private Resistance: John Calvin and Others on Breaking God's Rules." *Sixteenth Century Journal* 25:1 (1994): 3–27.

Tilly, Charles. "Reflections on the History of European State-Making." In *The Formation of National States in Western Europe.* Edited by Charles Tilly. Princeton: Princeton University Press, 1975.

Tomlin, Graham S. "The Medieval Origins of Luther's Theology of the Cross." *Archiv für Reformationsgeschichte* 89 (1998): 22–40.

Tonkin, John. *The Church and the Secular Order in Reformation Thought.* New York, Columbia University Press, 1971

Tracy, James D., ed. *Luther and the Modern State in Germany.* Kirksville: Sixteenth Century Journal Publishers, 1986.

Troeltsch, Ernst. *The Social Teaching of the Christian Churches.* 2 vols. Translated by Olive Wyon. New York: MacMillian, 1931. Repr., New York: Harper & Row, 1960.

Vercruyse, Jos. E. "Gesetz und Liebe, Die Struktur der 'Heidelberg Disputation' Luthers [1518]." *Lutherjahrbuch* 48 (1981): 7–43.

Watson, Philip S. *Let God Be God!: An Interpretation of the Theology of Martin Luther.* London: Epworth, 1947.

Whitford, David M. "John Adams, John Ponet and a Lutheran Influence on the American Revolution." *Lutheran Quarterly* XV.2 (2001): 143–58.

Willis-Watkins, [E.] David. "Calvin's Prophetic Reinterpretation of Kingship." In *Probing the Reformed Tradition: Historical Essays in Honor of Edward A. Dowey, Jr.* Louisville: Westminster/John Knox, 1989.

Wolgast, Eike. *Die Religionsfrage als Problem des Widerstandsrechts im 16. Jahrhundert.* Heidelberg: Carl Winter Universitätsverlag, 1980.

———. *Die Wittenberger Theologie und die Polik der evangelishen Stände: Studien zu Luthers Gutachten in Politik.* Gütersloh: Gütersloh Verlagshuas Mohn, 1977.

———. *Wegscheiden der Reformation: Alternative Denken vom 16 bis zum 18. Jahrhundert.* Weimar: Verlag Hermann Böhlaus Nachfolger, 1994.

Zachman, Randall C. *The Assurance of Faith: Conscience in the Theologies of Martin Luther and John Calvin.* Minneapolis: Fortress, 1993.

INDEX